THOMSON™

Here is your FREE access code to InfoTrac® College Edition
Only available with NEW copies of Thomson Higher Education textbooks

To open, detach at perforation

Use the access code inside this card to activate your

FREE 4-Month Subscription

Exclusively from Thomson Higher Education

DO NOT DISCARD
Your Access Code to Online Library Inside

STOP

www.infotrac-college.com

Changing the way the world learns®

Current Perspectives
Readings from InfoTrac® College Edition

To Accompany Rathus's Childhood and Adolescence: Voyages in Development, Second Edition

Current Perspectives
Readings from InfoTrac® College Edition

To Accompany Rathus's Childhood and Adolescence: Voyages in Development, Second Edition

DEBRA SCHWIESOW
Creighton University

Australia • Canada • Mexico • Singapore • Spain
United Kingdom • United States

Current Perspectives: Readings from InfoTrac® College Edition: To Accompany Rathus's Childhood and Adolescence: Voyages in Development, Second Edition
Debra Schwiesow

Senior Acquisitions Editor: *Michele Sordi*
Assistant Editor: *Dan Moneypenny*
Editorial Assistant: *Jessica Kim*
Marketing Manager: *Chris Caldeira*
Marketing Assistant: *Nicole Morinon*
Advertising Project Manager: *Tami Strang*
Project Manager, Editorial Production: *Christy Krueger*
Creative Director: *Robert Hugel*
Print Buyer: *Karen Hunt*
Production Service: *Rozi Harris, Interactive Composition Corporation*
Permissions Editor: *Kiely Sisk*
Cover Designer: *Larry Didona*
Cover Image: *Photolibrary.com/Photonica*
Cover and Text Printer: *Thomson West*
Compositor: *Interactive Composition Corporation*

© 2006 Thomson Wadsworth, a part of The Thomson Corporation. Thomson, the Star logo, and Wadsworth are trademarks used herein under license

ALL RIGHTS RESERVED. No part of this work covered by the copyright hereon may be reproduced or used in any form or by any means—graphic, electronic, or mechanical, including photocopying, recording, taping, Web distribution, information storage and retrieval systems, or in any other manner—without the written permission of the publisher.

Printed in the United States of America
2 3 4 5 6 7 09 08 07 06 05

For more information about our products, contact us at:
Thomson Learning Academic Resource Center
1-800-423-0563

For permission to use material from this text or product, submit a request online at http://www.thomsonrights.com.
Any additional questions about permissions can be submitted by email to thomsonrights@thomson.com.

Library of Congress Control Number: 2004117938

ISBN 0-495-00762-5

Thomson Higher Education
10 Davis Drive
Belmont, CA 94002-3098
USA

Asia (including India)
Thomson Learning
5 Shenton Way
#01-01 UIC Building
Singapore 068808

Australia/New Zealand
Thomson Learning Australia
102 Dodds Street
Southbank, Victoria 3006
Australia

Canada
Thomson Nelson
1120 Birchmount Road
Toronto, Ontario M1K 5G4
Canada

UK/Europe/Middle East/Africa
Thomson Learning
High Holborn House
50–51 Bedford Row
London WC1R 4LR
United Kingdom

Latin America
Thomson Learning
Seneca, 53
Colonia Polanco
11560 Mexico
D.F. Mexico

Spain (including Portugal)
Thomson Paraninfo
Calle Magallanes, 25
28015 Madrid, Spain

Contents

1

History, Theories, and Method

Piaget: The Man Who Listened to Children

Mavis Guinard

Jean Piaget was a Swiss child psychologist, sociologist, and philosopher whose works had a profound impact on child care and education. His studies on the origin, nature, and limits of human knowledge led him to formulate the theory that children do not think like adults and are only capable of gradually understanding concepts of volume, distance, numbers, and morality. Piaget conducted most of his studies on his three children who were observed while at play.

Jean Piaget, the renowned Swiss child psychologist, would have turned 100 on August 9, 1996. Last September, his centenary was celebrated by Geneva University with two scientific congresses, lectures and symposiums that attracted close to a thousand psychologists, educators and sociologists. France, the United States, South America, Eastern Europe and China were particularly well represented. An exhibit was geared to young visitors at Geneva's Museum of Ethnography at Conches while another in Neuchatel where Piaget was born, evoked his early years and training and a colloquium on Man and Time was set up in La Chaux-de-Fonds.

SwissWORLD, Feb–March 1997, n1, p21(2).

© 1997 SHZ Publications (Switzerland).

On hands and knees. Children don't think like grown ups, Jean Piaget found. Any mother might have told you that. But it took a Swiss scientist who, as a child watched birds and snails, then got on all fours to observe his own kids to make it dogma.

A child is not a small adult. Einstein said Piaget's discovery was "so simple only a genius could have thought of it". His lifelong research turned around this century's ideas on child care and education. While some fault Piaget for inspiring modern math, most praise his influence on the finest intention of parents and teachers: raising an active, self-reliant child.

Precocious. In 1906, on the way to school, ten-year-old Jean Piaget spotted a rare albino sparrow and dashed off half a dozen lines to a local scientific newsletter. This find "launched" him among European zoologists. At 15, he volunteered to catalogue mollusks at the Museum of Natural History in his home town of Neuchatel and was soon recognized as an authority. By 19, he had published 25 papers on alpine snails. Later, this made him a target for critics, who accused him of being a cold naturalist.

A convinced Darwinian, Piaget stuck to the theory that the simplest forms of life become in time more complex and adapt to surroundings. Struggling as an idealistic teenager to bridge the gap between science and faith, he was influenced by Henri Bergson's "Creative Evolution". The idea that human intelligence also may be triggered by evolution gripped him.

How humans learn. In 1918, after receiving a Ph.D. in natural science, Piaget moved to Zurich to study experimental psychology under Carl Jung. He then moved to Paris to study logic at the Sorbonne and abnormal psychology at the Salpetriere. In Alfred Binet's child psychology lab, he adapted Cyril Burt's true-false IQ tests to Paris schoolchildren. Not content to just add up errors, Piaget began to wonder why children of the same age groups made similar mistakes. Surprised by their reasoning, he realized that by observing and listening to children he might decode how humans learn.

Testing games. Back in Switzerland, the young scientist, now psychologist, sociologist and philosopher, began sixty years research in epistemology—a multi-disciplinary approach exploring the origin, nature and limits of human thinking. Many experiments were run in Geneva's "Maison des Petits", others on his three children, Lucienne, Jacqueline and Laurent. His wife, Valentine Chatenay, a former research assistant, took careful notes. Piaget's lifelong method was to observe normal children at play, scrupulously recording how they react or solve problems.

The games were fun. His children never resented them. Laurent Piaget once said, "I don't ever remember Father cross." The scientist who observed them from cradle to teens came to the conclusion that children only gradually grasp ideas of volume, distance, numbers and morality. It takes years before adult concepts make sense to a child.

How the mind grows. While he constantly widened his research, Piaget's aim, method and beliefs never changed. He pushed further and further to understand how the mind grows. Convinced a child's thinking evolves by adapting just as living creatures always adapted, he came to believe intelligence builds up between child and environment. Not all is innate, not all is learned. An active child learns in a stimulating environment; the most stimulating environment needs a child eager to respond.

This, Piaget could well understand. He grew up in an academic atmosphere—his father was a teacher of medieval literature—one which could be disrupted by his brilliant, yet neurotic mother. Piaget once said he escaped from family upheavals by hard work. It became therapy. "I am a worrier, only work relieves me," he once said.

Growth through understanding. He determined a child's mind grows in several stages. Baby meets the world through mouth, hands, eyes and clumsy motion. From two to seven, the infant embarks on the hard-on-parents age of discovery and has to accept that others may have different notions. Piaget saw the child under five utterly self-centred, using speech as running patter rather than communication. "Look, I'm drawing." In the next stage, from eight to eleven, a child's thinking is tied to the concrete but slowly acquires a sense of volume, a sense of time and a slightly skewed sense of justice. Not until the age of 12 do abstract reasoning and logic begin to develop.

Working first at Geneva's Jean-Jacques Rousseau Institute, then in Neuchatel, Piaget was named in 1929 professor of child psychology at Geneva University, a post held until 1980. Piaget left to others (teachers like Maria Montessori, children's writers like Delessert) to apply his findings. As head of the Bureau of International Education—later part of Unesco—he even warned against one universal type of education. "I don't believe in it. The only thing all systems have in common is the child himself," said the Swiss, aware that in his country, 26 cantons cling to 26 different school systems.

In Geneva he is thought to have gently suggested some secondary school reforms. But, like another Swiss genius, Le Corbusier, Piaget gained more followers abroad than at home. In 1955, he created the International Center for Genetic Epistemology to widen the scope of his research and attract other scientists working along the same lines. Called to the Sorbonne in 1952, his first lecture was on the relationship between love and intelligence in a child's development.

Books and honours. His first book, "The Language and Thought of the Child", was followed by over 50 works penned on a gloriously cluttered desk (many co-authored by collaborators). They were translated in 24 languages influencing child psychologists and educators around the world. Recognition earned him the Netherlands' coveted Erasmus prize and ten other international awards. After his first doctorate honoris causa from Harvard in 1936, he was offered 30 more from universities around the world.

Puffing on an eternal pipe, the man who listened to children remained a chubby, twinkling keen-eyed child at heart. In 1976, Piaget agreed to celebrate his 80th birthday defending his latest book in Geneva University before a jury and an audience of noted psychologists, many of them former students. "Since I never faced a single psychology exam but only a doctoral thesis on alpine snails," said Piaget, "I'm delighted to be given a chance to straighten out this scandalous situation." Because other academics were not amused the intended exam turned into a spirited intellectual joust. Piaget died four years later in 1980—a famed psychologist without a diploma.

CRITICAL THINKING QUESTIONS

1. What do you think is Piaget's greatest contribution to the field of child psychology? Why?
2. What implications do you think Piaget's work has for the education of children?
3. If you were conducting a seminar on Piagetian principles and had to limit your comments to three major topics, which ones would you choose and why?

2

Heredity and Conception

Pro & Con

Margaret Farley and Ruth Macklin

Should gender selection be used only in cases of medical need?

YES

The recent statement on sex selection from the American Society for Reproductive Medicine (ASRM) Ethics Committee says that, in general, efforts at sex selection for nonmedical reasons should be discouraged (*Fertil. Steril.* 72[4]:595–98, 1999).

As one of the authors, I believe that there are dangers to sex selection. Gender selection for nonmedical reasons should not be encouraged because of the potential problems of gender discrimination and misallocation of medical resources.

And to select a child primarily on the basis of gender seems to trivialize the meaning of the child overall.

Certainly, in other societies where different methods of sex selection have been used, such as infanticide or prenatal diagnosis and subsequent abortion, it has been clear that the predominantly favored gender has been selected.

OB GYN News, Dec 1, 1999, v34, i23, p9.

© 1999 International Medical News Group.

Although this is not so much a danger in the United States, we do live in a society characterized by sexism. So it's hard to believe that policies that condone sex selection and allocate medical resources for sex selection would not reinforce gender stereotypes.

The ASRM statement focuses specifically on the use of preimplantation genetic diagnosis (PGD) for sex selection. The most likely scenario would be when the embryo's sex is identified as part of or as a by-product of PGD performed for other medical reasons in a patient undergoing in vitro fertilization (IVF).

Another scenario occurs when the patient who is undergoing IVF and PGD requests that sex identification be added.

Or an infertility patient is undergoing IVF, and even though PGD is not necessary, the patient requests it solely for identifying the embryo's sex. These three applications of PGD should not be encouraged, because you still have the potential for some gender discrimination and inappropriate use and allocation of medical resources.

We come down harder on the practice of requesting IVF and PGD solely for the purpose of identifying the embryo's sex, which we say should be discouraged. This seems even more unreasonable because you add the burden of IVF as well as POD.

We refer to the method of prefertilization separation of X-bearing from Y-bearing sperm, which are then selected for artificial insemination or IVE We did not directly address this because we believed at the time that it was still investigational, but it now is available in at least one center.

When it is perfected, this method may cost less and certainly would not be as medically invasive as PGD, so it probably would not raise questions of misallocation of medical resources to the same degree. But this method still raises the issues of gender discrimination and the selection of offspring on the basis of nonessential human characteristics as well as questions regarding potential risks of the technique to offspring.

Margaret Farley, Ph.D., Gilbert L. Stark Professor of Christian Ethics, Yale University Divinity School, New Haven.

NO

The most ethically unproblematic justification for gender selection is people seeking to have a balanced family: They have one or more children of one sex and want a child of the opposite sex. That does not demonstrate any gender bias, and it's hard to see what kind of ethical reasons could be used to deny people that reproductive freedom. It doesn't violate anybody's rights, and it doesn't cause harm to anyone. We live in a country that permits reproductive freedom.

My position on whether something should be ethically permitted is to subject it to those two tests: Are anybody's rights violated and is anybody likely to be harmed? Indeed, it seems more likely that children born of the desired sex will benefit rather than be harmed.

These tests can be applied when the choice is to select the sex of the first child, which may raise questions of so called gender bias. But if 50% of the people offered this choice opt to have a girl first and 50% choose a boy first, no gender bias is exhibited; it's just individual preference. Under those circumstances, who would be harmed? One may argue that firstborn children have certain advantages because some literature suggests that firstborn children are more successful. But if it turned out that 50% choose a boy first and 50% choose a girl, it wouldn't be anything different from what nature provides. Then there would be no ethical reason to prohibit people from choosing the sex of their first child.

The next possibility is that many more people would choose boys as their first child. Then whose rights would be violated and who would be harmed? I argue nobody. Only if one believes that the firstborn has more advantages could you begin to make the case that those who choose boys would therefore disproportionally give male children an advantage. But I don't know how solid that evidence is. And there is countervailing evidence that there may be some advantages to being the youngest child.

The third scenario is to choose to have only girls or only boys. Many people would argue that to have such a preference is to have a gender bias and to have a gender bias is wrong. My response to this is that you're not going to eliminate the bias simply by saying it's wrong to have it. And people who have children of the unwanted sex may be disappointed and may convey that to the child in some way.

There is the argument that gender bias is such an important consideration that people should not be given the opportunity to exercise it. But why is gender bias—if indeed it results in a choice of not having the children of the preferred sex—any worse than choosing not to have a child with something like Down syndrome? If reproductive freedom allows people to choose against the gestation or birth of a child with a non-lethal birth defect, then why shouldn't the preference for a particular gender be just as acceptable?

Ruth Macklin, Ph.D., professor of bioethics, Albert Einstein College of Medicine, New York City.

CRITICAL THINKING QUESTIONS

1. Briefly summarize the arguments for the use of gender selection only when there is a medical need. Briefly summarize the arguments against.
2. What is your opinion? How do you think your opinions were formed on this issue?
3. What would ever consider the use of gender selection for yourself and your spouse? Under what conditions?

3

Prenatal Development

Drinking Moderately and Pregnancy

Joseph L. Jacobson and Sandra W. Jacobson

EFFECTS ON CHILD DEVELOPMENT

Moderate drinking(1) during pregnancy is associated with developmental problems in childhood that resemble but are less severe than the growth deficiencies and intellectual and behavioral impairment found among children with fetal alcohol syndrome (FAS). Children with FAS grow more slowly than do other children both before and after birth, exhibit intellectual and social problems, and display a distinctive pattern of abnormal facial features (Jones and Smith 1973). Intellectual and behavioral impairment are the most disabling characteristics of FAS. About one-half of all FAS patients are mentally retarded (i.e., they have an IQ below 70), and virtually all FAS patients exhibit serious attention and behavioral problems (Streissguth et al. 1991).

Several studies have found that children exposed to alcohol during pregnancy at lower levels than FAS children experience moderate intellectual and behavioral deficits that resemble those of FAS children but on a less severe level (Streissguth et al. 1993; Coles et al. 1997; Goldschmidt et al. 1996; J.L. Jacobson et al. 1996). Most of the mothers of children in these studies drank an average of 7 to 14 drinks per week (J.L. Jacobson and S.W. Jacobson 1994),

Alcohol Research & Health, Wntr 1999, v23, i1, p25.

© 1999 U.S. Government Printing Office.

a range generally considered as "moderate drinking." Although the deficits associated with full-blown FAS are devastating, the more subtle developmental problems associated with lower levels of prenatal alcohol exposure are far more prevalent among children than FAS. In response, researchers at the Institute of Medicine (IOM) have suggested a new medical term—"alcohol-related neurodevelopmental disorder" (ARND)—characterized by the intellectual and behavioral deficits experienced in alcohol-exposed, non-FAS children (Stratton et al. 1996).

This article summarizes the effects of moderate prenatal alcohol exposure on children's growth, intellectual competence, and behavior as well as discusses research findings regarding the impact of these effects on children's general ability to function. The article also investigates the doses and patterns of moderate drinking during pregnancy that have been linked to developmental problems in offspring.

EFFECTS ON GROWTH AS WELL AS INTELLECTUAL AND BEHAVIORAL FUNCTION

Children whose mothers drink moderately during pregnancy exhibit growth deficits as well as intellectual and behavioral impairment.

Growth

Although growth deficits are not a hallmark of ARND, consistent evidence indicates modest growth retardation in alcohol-exposed non-FAS infants before birth (e.g., Day et al. 1989; J.L. Jacobson et al. 1994a), and several studies have reported an association between prenatal alcohol exposure and slower-than-normal growth during the first 6 to 8 months after birth (J.L. Jacobson et al. 1994b). Moreover, deficits in height and head circumference have been documented in alcohol-exposed non-FAS children through age 6 (Day et al. 1994; also see Sampson et al. 1994). This slower growth pattern contrasts with the traditional finding that infants who weigh less at birth because of maternal smoking during pregnancy grow faster and tend to "catch up" during their first 5 to 6 months.

Intellectual Function

Unlike children with FAS, who frequently have reduced IQ scores, non-FAS alcohol-exposed children do not necessarily demonstrate IQ deficits (e.g., Goldschmidt et al. 1996; Coles et al. 1997; also see Streissguth et al. 1993). For example, one study failed to find an overall IQ deficit among non-FAS alcohol-exposed children but found that they exhibited poorer arithmetic, reading, and spelling skills than did non-alcohol-exposed children (Goldschmidt et al. 1996). Researchers have documented arithmetic and attention deficits both in FAS children (Streissguth et al. 1991) and in at least three groups of children with ARND—(1) a group of predominantly white, middle-class children in Seattle who were prenatally exposed to moderate amounts of alcohol (Streissguth et al. 1993), (2) a group of economically disadvantaged African-American children in Detroit whose mothers drank moderately during pregnancy (S.W. Jacobson et al. 1993), and (3) a group of disadvantaged African-American children in Atlanta who were prenatally exposed to moderate-to-heavy amounts of alcohol (Coles et al. 1997).

To measure attention deficits, researchers commonly use tests for the four attention components identified by Mirsky and colleagues (1991) (see table 1). (Table 1 and Illustrations referenced can be found within the online version of this article, at http://www.infotrac-college.com.) Sustained attention refers to the child's ability to maintain focused concentration and alertness over time. Focused attention is a measure of the length of time the child maintains attention in the presence of distractions. Executive function involves the child's ability to coordinate, plan, and execute appropriate responses and modify his or her behavior in response to feedback. Working memory is a measure of the child's ability to mentally manipulate the information presented and to link this information with other information retrieved from memory.

Although research has documented low levels of sustained attention (Streissguth et al. 1993), focused attention (Streissguth et al. 1994), and executive function (Coles et al. 1997) in ARND children, these children's most consistent deficits are in working memory. Streissguth and colleagues (1993) found that the two strongest negative effects observed in ARND children at age 7 were on arithmetic tests and the Digit Span test (which assesses the child's ability to remember strings of digits); both are IQ subtests that depend most heavily on working memory. The two neuropsychological tests most strongly affected—the Children's Memory Test (which assesses recall of details from stories read aloud to the child) and Seashore Rhythm (which assess the ability to discriminate between pairs of rhythmic patterns)—also measure working memory (Streissguth et al. 1993). Deficits on two working memory tests, the Stepping Stone Maze (which assesses the ability to find and recall an invisible path by moving a cursor through a matrix of squares) and Seashore Rhythm, also were among the strongest effects seen at age 14 (Streissguth et al. 1994). Similarly, S.W. Jacobson and colleagues (1998b) found that at age 7.5, the strongest effects were seen on arithmetic and Digit Span tests and timed tasks entailing mental manipulation of information, such as mental rotation (see table 1). Coles and colleagues (1997) also found that working memory impairments were among the strongest effects observed at 7.5 years.

Researchers have corroborated these effects on working memory in laboratory animal experiments, which have linked prenatal alcohol exposure to impaired performance on the Morris water maze (which assesses the animal's ability to find and recall the location of a platform submerged in an opaque liquid) (Hannigan et al. 1993) and on the radial eight-arm maze (which assesses the animal's ability to retrieve food pellets from the end of all eight arms of a maze without revisiting arms from which food has already been retrieved) at both moderate (Reyes et al. 1989) and heavy (Hall et al. 1994) levels of alcohol exposure.

Behavioral Function

In addition to the intellectual and attention deficits found among non-FAS alcohol-exposed-children, researchers also have documented behavior problems that resemble but are less severe than those found among FAS children. The socialization deficits associated with FAS include poor interpersonal skills and an inability to conform to social conventions (Streissguth 1997). Streissguth has described FAS patients as being "unaware of the consequences of [their] behavior, especially the social consequences," showing "poor judgment in whom to trust," and unable to "take a hint [i.e., needing strong clear commands]" (p. 127).

Relatively limited information is available regarding behavioral effects in alcohol-exposed non-FAS children. Using the Achenbach Child Behavior Checklist-Teacher's Report Form (TRF), Brown and colleagues (1991) found poorer social competence and more aggressive and destructive behavior in children whose mothers drank throughout their pregnancies than in children whose mothers had stopped drinking in mid-pregnancy or abstained during pregnancy, independent of current maternal drinking patterns. In another study, prenatal alcohol exposure was associated with higher teacher ratings in three of the eight TRF problem areas—social, attention, and aggression—and greater inattention and impulsivity on the DuPaul-Barkley Attention Deficit Hyperactivity Disorder (ADHD) Scale, after controlling for potential confounding factors such as maternal smoking during pregnancy, quality of parenting, and current caregiver drinking (S.W. Jacobson et al. 1998a). Analyses showed that the social, aggression, and impulsivity problems were not merely by-products of the children's attention deficits, indicating that alcohol directly affects diverse aspects of central nervous system function. A high proportion of children had problems in the borderline or clinical range. For example, 33 percent of the children prenatally exposed to moderate or heavy levels of alcohol exhibited aggressive behavior problems of this magnitude, compared with only 4 to 5 percent of the general population. One study found that at age 14, children with higher levels of prenatal alcohol exposure were more likely to have negative feelings about themselves; to be aggressive and delinquent; and to use alcohol, tobacco, and other drugs (Carmichael Olson et al. 1997).

EFFECTS ON CHILDREN'S DAY-TO-DAY FUNCTION

The effects of moderate prenatal alcohol exposure on children's intellectual performance and behavior have been established. When examining the results of psychological tests, however, children with ARND often appear to have relatively subtle impairments (i.e., their average test scores are no more than a few points below normal). Although the average effect may be small, researchers have recently begun to examine whether the effects of moderate drinking are severe enough in certain children to affect their ability to manage on a day-to-day basis at school, home, and with peers.

To evaluate whether a specific deficit is severe enough to impair a child's day-to-day function, researchers must establish criteria to indicate which test scores are low enough to be functionally significant (i.e., indicating a deficit severe enough to interfere with the ability to manage in school and other social contexts). For example, an IQ below 70 indicates mental retardation, but little consensus exists regarding the functional importance of a 5- or 10-point decrement when scores fall within the normal range. Moreover, for most psychological tests, such as those focusing on attention, no criteria for functional significance have been established, limiting the ability to evaluate the effect of ARND on children's everyday function. In the absence of established criteria, Streissguth and colleagues (1993) used the bottom 7.5 percentile of scores to identify the children with the greatest deficiencies, and J.L. Jacobson and colleagues (1998) have used the bottom 10th percentile to indicate "poor performance." These criteria are based on the premise that although the children's performance at these levels may fall within the normal range, the performance levels are poor enough that they likely interfere with the children's day-to-day functioning.

To determine whether the ARND children in one study had deficits that could be considered functionally significant, the researchers evaluated the children's performance at approximately 12 months of age on four measures: (1) the Bayley Mental Index, which assesses simple fine motor and prehensile coordination (e.g., grasping a pencil and placing wood pieces in a puzzle) and imitation of a model; (2) the Bayley Psychomotor Index, which assesses walking and balance; (3) elicited play, which determines the most complex play with toys a child can imitate (e.g., placing a lid securely on a teapot or pretending to drink from a cup); and (4) cognitive processing speed, a measure of how quickly a child processes information, which is assessed by measuring the average length of the glances the child directs at an object or photograph (S.W. Jacobson et al. 1993). Children who scored in the bottom 10th percentile on a given outcome were considered to have a functionally significant deficit in that outcome.

The researchers then examined the association between the mothers' alcohol consumption and the rates of functionally significant impairment in the children of both younger and older mothers. For the first three measures, mothers under age 30 did not appear to put their children at increased risk for functional impairment by drinking seven or more drinks per week (see J.L. Jacobson and colleagues [1998] for a discussion of the basis for the seven-drink-per-week threshold). For infants born to older women (i.e., age 30 and over), however, drinking above the threshold was associated with a three- to fivefold increase in functional impairment. For the fourth outcome, processing speed, drinking above the threshold doubled the risk of functional deficit in children of mothers in both age groups (i.e., the more heavily exposed children were statistically more likely to exhibit a functional deficit when the data in the two maternal age groups were pooled).

These findings are consistent with data from case studies of multiparous alcohol-abusing mothers of FAS children, which have shown that each successive child is almost always more severely impaired than the previous one. Similarly, animal experiments in which the doses of prenatal alcohol exposure were carefully controlled have documented markedly greater impairment in offspring born to older mothers.

PATTERN OF MATERNAL DRINKING DURING PREGNANCY

Most existing data on the effects seen in non-FAS alcohol-exposed children have been based on each of the mother's alcohol intake averaged across her pregnancy. However, animal experiments indicate that this average is probably misleading, because ingesting a given dose of alcohol over a short time period (i.e., within a few hours) generates a greater peak blood alcohol concentration (BAC) and greater neuronal and behavioral impairment than does ingesting the same dose gradually over several days (Bonthius and West 1990).

The authors reanalyzed the infant data to examine the effects of dose (i.e., the average number of drinks per drinking occasion) and frequency (i.e., the average days per week of drinking during pregnancy) on developmental outcome (J.L. Jacobson et al. 1998). Children who scored in the bottom 10th percentile on one or more of the four outcomes in the figure were considered to be functionally impaired. As shown in table 2, 16 of the 20 functionally impaired infants (i.e., 80 percent) were born to women who drank on average at least five drinks per occasion during pregnancy (see table 2).

Ninety-one percent of the mothers in the study drank infrequently (i.e., no more than 2 days per week). Among the 11 infants in the sample whose mothers drank frequently (i.e., at least 4 days per week) during pregnancy, functional impairment was seen in 4 of the 5 infants whose mothers averaged at least 5 drinks per occasion but in none of the 6 infants whose mothers drank frequently at lower levels (ranging from 1.3 to 4.6 drinks per occasion). The

Table 2. Relation of Alcohol Dose per Occasion During Pregnancy to Incidence of Functionally Significant Deficit in Offspring During Infancy(*)

	Drinks per Occasion	
Functional Deficit	< 5	≥ 5
Yes	4 (21%)	16 (57%)
No	15 (79%)	12 (43%)
Total children	19 (100%)	28 (100%)

* N = 47.

NOTES: Only mothers who averaged at least seven drinks per week during pregnancy were included in this analysis. The relation shown in the table is statistically significant at $p < 0.025$.

Source: J.L. Jacobson et al. 1998.

one mother who drank daily was an alcoholic, and her infant was born with FAS. However, the infant of the frequently drinking mother who averaged only 1.3 drinks per occasion showed no evidence of neurodevelopmental impairment. The median drinking pattern of the mothers of the 20 children in table 2 with functional impairment was 7 drinks per occasion on 1 to 2 days per week. Although 7 to 14 drinks per week is often considered "moderate" drinking, this pattern of infrequent heavy doses may be characterized more accurately as heavy weekend drinking.

CONCLUSIONS

Several studies have found that moderate prenatal alcohol exposure has statistically significant effects on children's cognitive and behavioral development. Using the IOM-proposed terminology, many of these children would be diagnosed as having ARND. ARND differs from FAS, however, in that FAS is characterized by reduced IQ scores and more severe socialization problems. Nevertheless, evaluations of the specific domains in which deficits occur reveal important parallels between FAS and ARND. In the cognitive domain, arithmetic, attention, and working memory are most severely and consistently affected in both disorders. In the behavioral domain, both disorders are marked by increased impulsivity, aggression, and social problems. Researchers are only beginning to address the importance of these deficits for the day-to-day functioning of the ARND child. The aforementioned data suggest that although some non-FAS alcohol-exposed children are only minimally affected by prenatal alcohol exposure, other more susceptible children are impaired to a degree likely to interfere with their ability to function normally. Detailed information about the functional significance of each of the deficits found among ARND children is needed to fully understand the implications of prenatal alcohol exposure for child development.

More attention also should be devoted to determining the specific drinking levels and patterns associated with functionally significant developmental impairment. Research has documented functionally significant deficits in infants whose mothers drank, on average, five or more drinks per occasion once or twice per week. Although considered excessive for a pregnant woman, this level of drinking falls short of the rate usually associated with having a serious drinking problem. Given the marked individual differences in alcohol metabolism and fetal vulnerability, five drinks per occasion may be too high a threshold for many women. Functional deficits may occur in some children who are repeatedly exposed prenatally to only three or four drinks per occasion, especially if the alcohol is consumed on an empty stomach. In evaluating the risk associated with exposure to environmental and food contaminants, a safety margin is usually incorporated to allow for individual differences in sensitivity. Where human data are available, a safety factor of 10 is used for this purpose (Sette and Levine 1986). Using this approach, researchers might divide the threshold value of seven drinks per week that is often found for the neurobehavioral effects of alcohol (J.L. Jacobson and S.W. Jacobson 1994) by 10 and conclude that 0.7 drinks per week (one drink every 10 days) is likely considered to be "safe" drinking. Obstetrical care providers can reassure patients who have consumed a few alcoholic beverages once or twice early in their pregnancies that they need not be overly concerned.

These data demonstrate a statistically significant association between moderate drinking during pregnancy and children's adverse neurobehavioral outcomes. The data also demonstrate that these effects may be severe enough in some children to affect their day-to-day functioning. Although children exposed to moderate levels of alcohol during pregnancy are not mentally retarded, they show attention deficits and behavioral problems that are similar to, although less severe than, those found in FAS children. These data also demonstrate that as with most neurotoxicants, the human organism is markedly more vulnerable to alcohol exposure during the prenatal period than at any other point in the lifespan. Because of this heightened vulnerability and the apparently long-term, permanent nature of alcohol-related deficits, the best advice continues to be abstinence or, at most, minimal consumption of alcohol during pregnancy.

NOTES

1. Definitions of moderate drinking vary. For the purposes of this article, 7 to 14 drinks per week is considered moderate drinking. The Federal government has adopted more conservative guidelines, defining moderate drinking as no more than one drink per day for women and

no more than two drinks per day for men (U.S. Department of Agriculture and the U.S. Department of Health and Human Services 1995).

2. Most IQ tests have a mean of 100 (i.e., 100 is considered normal) and a standard deviation of 15 points. An IQ of less than 70 is usually considered to indicate mental retardation, and IQ scores of 70 to 79 are considered to indicate borderline mental retardation.

CRITICAL THINKING QUESTIONS

1. In your own words summarize the purpose of this research and the major findings. In your opinion what are the two most important findings? Why?
2. In your opinion what are the most detrimental effects alcohol may have on a child? Are your opinions supported by what you read in this article?
3. Can you identify any problems with the design or findings of this research? If so, how might you redesign it to correct for any of these problems?
4. What advice would you give an expectant mother regarding the use of alcohol based on the findings of this research?

REFERENCES

Bonthius, D.J., and West, J.R. Alcohol-induced neuronal loss in developing rats: Increased brain damage with binge exposure. *Alcoholism: Clinical and Experimental Research* 14(1):107–118, 1990.

Brown, R.T.; Coles, C.D.; Smith, I.E.; Platzman, K.A.; Silverstein, J.; Erickson, S., and Falek, A. Effects of prenatal alcohol exposure at school age: II. Attention and behavior. *Neurotoxicology and Teratology* 13(4): 369–376, 1991.

Carmichael Olson, H.; Streissguth, A.P.; Sampson, P.D.; Barr, H.M.; Bookstein, F.L.; and Thiede, K. Association of prenatal alcohol exposure with behavioral and learning problems in early adolescence. *Journal of the American Academy of Child and Adolescent Psychiatry* 36(9):1187–1194, 1997.

Coles, C.D.; Platzman, K.A.; Raskind-Hood, C.L.; Brown, R.T.; Falek, A.; and Smith, I.E. A comparison of children affected by prenatal alcohol exposure and attention deficit hyperactivity disorder. *Alcoholism: Clinical and Experimental Research* 20(1):150–161, 1997.

Day, N.L.; Jasperse, D.; Richardson, G.; Robles, N.; Sambamoorthi, U.; Taylor, P.; Scher, M.; Stoffer, D.; and Cornelius, M. Prenatal exposure to alcohol: Effect on infant growth and morphologic characteristics. *Pediatrics* 84(3):536–541, 1989.

Day, N.L.; Richardson, G.A.; Geva, D.; and Robles, N. Alcohol, marijuana and tobacco: The effects of prenatal exposure on offspring growth and morphology at age six. *Alcoholism: Clinical and Experimental Research* 18(4):786–794, 1994.

Goldschmidt, L.; Richardson, G.A.; Stoffer, D.S.; Geva, D.; and Day, N.L. Prenatal alcohol exposure and academic achievement at age six: A nonlinear fit. *Alcoholism: Clinical and Experimental Research* 20(4):763–770, 1996.

Hall, J.L.; Church, MW.; and Berman, R.F. Radial arm maze deficits in rats exposed to alcohol during midgestation. *Psychobiology* 22(3): 181–185, 1994.

Hannigan, J.H.; Berman, R.F.; and Zajac, C.S. Environmental enrichment and the behavioral effects of prenatal exposure to alcohol in rats. *Neurotoxicology and Teratology* 15(4):261–266, 1993.

Jacobson, J.L., and Jacobson, S.W. Prenatal alcohol exposure and neurobehavioral development: Where is the threshold? *Alcohol Health & Research World* 18(1):30–36, 1994.

Jacobson, J.L.; Jacobson, S.W.; Sokol, R.J.; Martier, S.S.; Ager, J.W.; and Shankaran, S. Effects of alcohol use, smoking, and illicit drug use on fetal growth in black infants. *Journal of Pediatrics* 124(5) (Part 1):757–764, 1994a.

Jacobson, J.L.; Jacobson, S.W.; and Sokol, R.J. Effects of prenatal exposure to alcohol, smoking, and illicit drugs on postpartum somatic growth. *Alcoholism: Clinical and Experimental Research* 18(2):317–323, 1994b.

Jacobson, J.L.; Jacobson, S.W.; and Sokol, R.J. Increased vulnerability to alcohol-related birth defects in the offspring of mothers over 30. *Alcoholism: Clinical and Experimental Research* 20(2):359–363, 1996.

Jacobson, J.L.; Jacobson, S.W.; Sokol, R.J.; and Ager, J.W. Relation of maternal age and pattern of pregnancy drinking to functionally significant cognitive deficit in infancy. *Alcoholism: Clinical and Experimental Research* 22(2):345–351, 1998.

Jacobson, S.W.; Jacobson, J.L.; and Sokol, R.J.; Martier, S.S.; and Ager, T.W. Prenatal alcohol exposure and infant information processing ability. *Child Development* 64(6):1706–1721, 1993.

Jacobson, S.W.; Jacobson, J.L.; Sokol, R.J.; and Chiodo, L.M. Preliminary evidence of primary socioemotional deficits in 7-year-olds prenatally exposed to alcohol. *Alcoholism: Clinical and Experimental Research* 22:61A, 1998a.

Jacobson, S.W.; Jacobson, J.L.; Sokol, R.J.; Chiodo, L.M.; Berube, R.L.; and Narang, S. Preliminary evidence of working memory and attention deficits in 7-year-olds prenatally exposed to alcohol. *Alcoholism: Clinical and Experimental Research* 22: 61A, 1998b.

Jones, K.L., and Smith, D.W. Recognition of the fetal alcohol syndrome in early infancy. *Lancet* 2(7836):999–1001, 1973.

Mirsky, A.F.; Anthony, B.J.; Duncan, C.C.; Ahearn, M.B.; and Kellam, S.G. Analysis of the elements of attention: A neuropsychological approach. *Neuropsychology Review* 2:109–145, 1991.

Reyes, E.; Wolfe, J.; and Savace, D.D. The effects of prenatal alcohol exposure on radial arm maze performance in adult rats. *Physiology and Behavior* 46(1):45–48, 1989.

Sampson, P.D.; Bookstein, F.L.; Barr, H.M.; and Streissguth, A.P. Prenatal alcohol exposure, birthweight, and measures of child size from birth to age 14 years. *American Journal of Public Health* 84(9):1421–1428, 1994.

Sette, W.F., and Levine, T.E. Behavior as a regulatory endpoint. In: Annau, Z., ed. *Neurobehavioral Toxicology*. Baltimore: Johns Hopkins Press, 1986. pp. 391–403.

Stratton, K.; Howe, C.; and Battaglia, F., eds. *Fetal Alcohol Syndrome: Diagnosis, Epidemiology, Prevention, and Treatment*. Washington, DC: National Academy Press, 1996.

Streissguth, A.P. *Fetal Alcohol Syndrome: A Guide for Families and Communities.* Baltimore: Paul H. Brookes Publishing, 1997.

Streissguth, A.P.; Aase, J.M.; Clarren, S.K.; Randels, S.P.; Ladue, R.A.; and Smith, D.F. Fetal alcohol syndrome in adolescents and adults. Journal of the American Medical Association 265(15):1961–1967, 1991.

Streissguth, A.P.; Bookstein, F.L.; Sampson, P.D.; and Barr, H.M. *The Enduring Effects of Prenatal Alcohol Exposure on Child Development: Birth Through 7 Years, a Partial Least squares Solution.* Ann Arbor: University of Michigan Press, 1993.

Streissguth, A.P.; Sampson, P.D.; Carmichael Olson, H.; Bookstein, F.L.; Barr, H.M.; Scott, M.; Feldman, J.; and Mirsky, A.F. Maternal drinking during pregnancy: Attention and short-term memory in 14-year-old offspring—A longitudinal prospective study. *Alcoholism: Clinical and Experimental Research* 18(1):202–218, 1994.

U.S. Department of Agriculture and the U.S. Department of Health and Human Services. *Nutrition and Your Health: Dietary Guidelines for Americans.* 4th ed. Washington, DC: Department of Health and Human Services, 1995.

Joseph L. Jacobson, Ph.D., is a professor in the Department of Psychology, College of Science, and Sandra W. Jacobson, Ph.D., is a professor in the Department of Psychiatry and Behavioral Neurosciences, School of Medicine, Wayne State University, Detroit, Michigan.

Research and preparation of this article were supported by National Institute on Alcohol Abuse and Alcoholism grants R01-AA06966, P50-AA07607, and R01-AA09524.

4

Birth and the Newborn Baby: In the New World

Postnatal Depression

Cheryll Adams

The symptoms of postnatal depression are not always obvious and an awareness of risk factors that may determine mental health outcomes is vital.

KEY POINTS

- Postnatal depression is more likely to be triggered by life circumstances than by hormonal disturbance
- Research suggests that antenatal depression is almost as common
- Practice nurses can play a vital role in initiating a package of care and support
- The term postnatal depression describes a mild to moderate non-psychotic depression that affects 100–150 mothers in every 1000 during the postnatal year. It is most common in the first 3 months following their baby's birth. (1,2)
- Although there is little evidence that it differs from depression at any other time, it is particularly significant at this stage in a family's lifecycle. The mother has a young baby to care for and is herself vulnerable due to the challenges of new motherhood.

Practice Nurse, June 27, 2003, v25, i12, p44(4).

© 2003 Reed Health Communications Ltd.

CAUSES

For many years there has been a commonly held belief that hormonal disturbance is responsible for postnatal depression but there is little research evidence to back this up. It seems much more likely that it is triggered by life circumstances. One study demonstrated that a persistently crying baby can trigger a depression. (3)

The main risk factors for postnatal depression seem to be: (4)

- a history of psychopathology and psychological disturbance during pregnancy
- poor social support
- a poor relationship with the father of the baby
- recent stressful events
- persistent baby blues

The media images of happy, healthy, smiling, celebrity mothers with slim figures, defy the reality of motherhood for most women who do not have the luxury of personal trainers and nannies to support them.

Women can experience a sense of failure and also guilt that they are feeling depressed when the world seems to expect them to be happy. A common fear among mothers is that if they tell a professional that they are not coping then their baby may be taken away.

WIDER IMPLICATIONS

As well as affecting the mother, postnatal depression can also have profound effects on her baby, her other children and her marriage. Longitudinal studies have demonstrated that postnatal depression can result in insecure attachment between the baby and the mother, which may affect the child's psychological, social and educational development. Sons of depressed mothers, in particular, have been shown to be more likely to have lower intelligence quotients. (5, 6, 7, 8)

These wider implications are likely to be more apparent when the mother is unsupported, in an insecure relationship or is living in poverty.

PRESENTATION

Women with postnatal depression may not display obvious symptoms and you may only realise that something is wrong when you ask them how they are feeling. The most common symptoms of postnatal depression are:

- a loss of pleasure or interest in life
- a low mood, sadness, tearfulness

- exhaustion that is not relieved by sleep
- feelings of guilt
- irritability
- poor concentration
- loss of confidence
- anxiety
- sleep difficulties
- a dreadful sense of isolation

THE ROLE OF THE PRACTICE NURSE

Many mothers will be seen by the practice nurse during their pregnancy, as well as during the postnatal period. The practice nurse may know the woman better than the midwife and would be more likely to be aware of risk factors and other circumstances that may determine her mental health outcome after the baby's birth. Issues such as recent family bereavement, partner's unemployment, the pregnancy being unwanted or a history of domestic violence are all significant.

About 10–15% of the mothers attending immunisation clinics may have the condition and practice nurses can play a vital role in helping identify them and initiating a package of care and support.

The practice nurse should ideally discuss any such concerns with the mother and encourage her to talk about them with her midwife or health visitor. If this is not possible she can alert the midwife, GP or health visitor to the fact that there are issues in the woman's life that may make her vulnerable to mental illness. This ensures that the mother gets additional support without needing to break confidentiality about sensitive situations.

A practice nurse who knows a mother well may quickly be aware that all is not well postnatally. There isn't much time during an immunisation session to focus on the mother, but even a brief enquiry such as "How are you?" could be very important in supporting the early mobilisation of help.

ANTENATAL MOOD DISTURBANCE

Researchers have recently discovered that depression may be almost as common antenatally as postnatally and may cause adverse effects such as premature labour and small-for-dates babies. (9, 10)

There is also some evidence to suggest it may be associated with behavioural problems at the age of 4. (11)

It is important to assess mood of any woman seen during pregnancy, even if time limits this to asking "How are you feeling?" You also need to determine for how long the mother's mood has been disturbed. Everyone has 'off days' but a woman who has been feeling low or anxious for some time can be advised to discuss how she is feeling with her partner, a relative or a friend. If necessary she could be guided to speak to the midwife, GP or health visitor.

MANAGEMENT

The Government has recognised the importance of maternal mental health and advises a care pathway approach with every primary care trust having a strategy for its management. (1, 2, 3) Successful NHS interventions include, cognitive behavioural therapy and counselling delivered by health visitors, attendance at therapeutic groups and medication such as SSRIs or tricyclics. If a mother is breastfeeding, care must be taken in the choice of antidepressant and many mothers favour non-pharmaceutical treatments. The voluntary sector can also play a useful part by supporting mothers and families when the mother is depressed through schemes such as HomeStart.

Managing postnatal depression in the community needs to be the responsibility of the whole primary healthcare team with support from the mental health services in more severe cases. Mental health professionals can also play an important role in providing training and supervision. Midwives and health visitors have a specific responsibility to seek out women who may be depressed or at risk of depression but they need the support of other members of the team. If the potentially serious outcomes from antenatal and postnatal depression are to be prevented it is important that the practice nurse supports her primary care colleagues by being alert to those mothers who are vulnerable so that interventions can be started early. As is so often the case in healthcare the key is good communication.

THE BABY BLUES AND PUERPERAL PSYCHOSIS

This article concentrates on postnatal depression but it is also important to be aware of the two other types of depression affecting mothers:

Baby Blues

This affects about 80% of mothers and is normally transient. It consists of a brief period of tearfulness occurring around the third day fallowing birth.

If the 'blues' persist beyond a few days it may be cause for concern as it suggests that the mother is clinically depressed.

Puerperal Psychosis

This affects 1–2 mothers in every 1000 during the postnatal year. It is a serious psychiatric condition with symptoms such as a loss of contact with reality, hallucinations and abnormal behaviour.

Normally the onset is in the first few days post delivery, sometimes when the mother is still in hospital, though it may present later.

It requires urgent referral and usually hospitalisation.

Mothers who have experienced a previous serious psychiatric illness are some of those most vulnerable to suffering with puerperal psychosis.

Cheryll Adams MSc, BSc, DMS, RN, RHV is a professional officer with the Community Practitioners' and Health Visitors' Association.

FURTHER READING

- Scottish Intercollegiate Guideline no 60. Postnatal Depression and Puerperal Psychosis which can be downloaded from the website: www.sign.ac.uk.
- Community Practitioners' and Health Visitors' Association (CPHVA) *Postnatal Depression and Maternal Mental Health, a public health priority.* London: CPHVA, 2001.
- Nicolson P. *Postnatal depression: facing the paradox of loss, happiness and motherhood.* Chichester: Wiley, 2001.
- Heather Welford. *Feelings afterbirth.* London: The National Childbirth Trust, 2002.

CRITICAL THINKING QUESTIONS

1. What are some of the common symptoms and suspected causes of postnatal depression?
2. Why could depression after the birth of a child be more detrimental than depression at another time in a mother's or a child's life?
3. What are some recommendations made by the author regarding diagnosis and treatment of postnatal depression? What other recommendations would you add?

REFERENCES

1. O'Hara M, Swain A. Rates and risk of postnatal depression—a meta-analysis. *Int Rev Psychiatry* 1996; 8: 37–73.
2. Cox J, Murray D, Chapman G. A controlled study of the onset, duration and prevalence of postnatal depression. *Br J Psychiatry* 1993; 163: 27–31.

3. Murray L, Stanley C, Hooper R, King F, FioriCowley A. The role of infant factors in postnatal depression and mother-infant interactions. *Der Med Child Neurol* 1996; 38[2]: 109–119.

4. Scottish Intercollegiate Guidelines Network. *Postnatal Depression and Puerperal Psychosis: a national clinical guideline.* Edinburgh: SIGN, 2002.

5. Murray L. How postnatal depression can affect children and their families. In: *Postnatal Depression and maternal mental health a public health priority.* London: CPHVA, 2001.

6. Hay D, Pawlby S, Sharp D, Asten P, Mills A, Kumar R. Intellectual Problems Shown by 11 Year Old Children Whose Mothers Had Postnatal Depression. *J Child Psychol Psychiatry* 2001; 42: 871–90.

7. Boath Eh, Pryce AJ and Cox JL. Postnatal depression: the impact on the family. *J of Reproductive and Infant Psychology* 1998; 16[2/3]: 199–213.

8. Sharp D, Hay D, Pawlby S, Schmucker G, Allen H, Kumar R. The impact of postnatal depression on boys' intellectual development. *J Child Psychol Psychiatry* 1995; 36: 1315–37.

9. Evans J, Heron J, Francomb H, Oke S, Golding J. Cohort study of depressed mood during pregnancy and after childbirth. *Br Med J* 2001; 323: 257–60.

10. Copper R, Goldenber R, Das A, Elder N, Swain M, Norman G et al. The preterm prediction study: maternal stress is associated with spontaneous preterm birth at less than thirty five weeks gestation. *Am J Obstet Gyneco* 1996; 175: 1286–92.

11. Glover V. Antenatal and postnatal mood: the effects on the fetus and child. In: *Postnatal Depression and maternal mental health a public health priority.* London: CPHVA, 2001.

12. Department of Health. *National Service Framework for Mental Health.* London: HMSO, 1999.

13. Department of Health. *Women's mental health: into the mainstream—strategic development of mental health care for women.* London: DoH, 2002.

5

Infancy: Physical Development

Infant Nutrition in the First Year of Life: Tradition or Science?

Christina J. Calamaro

All pediatric nurses understand the importance of optimal nutrition for the normal healthy child. The nurse knows that in order for children of all ages to reach the goal of adequate nutrition, up-to-date advice and dietary support must be provided. The body of knowledge in pediatric clinical nutrition has seen great advances over the past few decades. Current nutritional recommendations are well publicized, yet many of these guidelines are not scientifically based, leaving many pediatric nurses as well as care givers with questions about what is and what is not proper nutrition for the child.

Caregivers also have many questions ranging from how to begin various solids, to the order in which foods should be introduced, to what foods should be avoided. The pediatric primary care nurse is in a key position to educate the caregiver about pediatric nutrition, as he or she sees the child frequently during the early years of life. It is imperative to teach healthy dietary behavior during the first years of life, since these are the years of greatest growth, physically as well as developmentally. Assisting the caregivers to understand the importance of

Pediatric Nursing, March 2000, v26, i2, p211.

© 2000 Jannetti Publications, Inc.

age-appropriate nutrition can help to establish healthy dietary habits into adulthood, it is a priority, therefore, for the pediatric nurse to be aware of any changes in pediatric nutrition in order to provide factual, evidence-based, nutritional teaching. In order to explain infant nutrition and provide successful teaching to caregivers, the nurse needs to understand the history of infant feeding and how current recommendations have evolved.

BREAST AND BOTTLE FEEDING DURING INFANCY

Breastfeeding was once the primary source of nutrition for the infant. Historically, feeding practices up through the 19th and early 20th century included breastfeeding well into the second year of life (Hammer, Bryson, & Agras, 1999). In the United States up until the 1920s, solid food was seldom recommended before age 1 year. If an infant could not tolerate breastmilk, goat's milk or "cereal Pap" (a semi-solid liquid preparation) was given (American Academy of Pediatrics [AAP], 1997). With industrialization came emancipation for women and opportunities for women in the workforce. At the time of World War II, as women moved into the job market, breastfeeding became a difficult option because of extended time periods away from the child. Bottle feeding with cow's or goat's milk or evaporated milk were the only choices.

Industrialization not only provided a change in the role of women, but also produced advances in medicine and science. These advances led to an increase in the variety of infant formulas and foods. Cow's milk or evaporated milk were no longer the only options; newly developed formulas provided healthier alternatives.

As more women chose the convenience of bottle-feeding, the number of breastfed infants decreased. By 1970, only 30% of women in the United States were breastfeeding their infants at 1 week of age (Oski, 1994). This trend was also witnessed in other industrialized nations. In the United Kingdom, the prevalence of breastfeeding a 6-month-old had fallen to 9% (Gale & Martyn, 1996). By the beginning of the 1990s, only 49% of women were breastfeeding their infants, opting for infant formula as the primary source of nutrition (Riordan, 1997). A national objective and goal of Healthy People 2000 is to "increase to at least 75% the proportion of mothers who breastfeed their babies in the early postpartum period and to at least 50% the proportion who continue breastfeeding until their babies are 5 to 6 months old" (United States Public Health Service [USPHS], 1999).

In the 1970s, children of families with incomes below the poverty line were discovered to be smaller in height and weight. They also had a prevalence of anemia, estimated at 20% to 30% (Owen & Owen, 1997). The Special Supplemental Nutritional Program for Women, Infants, and Children (WIC) was legislated in 1972 to address this grave health concern. The health of pregnant women and children living in poverty improved dramatically because the planners of WIC combined food supplementation with nutritional education. Iron-fortified infant formula and other supplemental foods to enrich the diet of young children and pregnant mothers were provided via grocery store vouchers.

With the availability of health foods and formulas, immediate improvement in the health of this population was documented. Not only were there lower incidences of maternal anemia, decreased prevalence of low-birth-weight infants, and better growth in children, but effective reduction of toddler and preschool iron deficiency anemia occurred (Owen & Owen, 1997). By the mid-1980s, half of the eligible infants born in the United States were participating in WIC; 75% of those infants were formula fed (Owen & Owen, 1997). With the onset of WIC and the easy availability of iron fortified infant formula, low birth weight and iron deficiency anemia have been reduced. A question continues regarding the correlation between the development of WIC and the lower breastfeeding rates of the lower socioeconomic population from the 1970s up through today.

Seeing the decline of breastfeeding mothers, the AAP decided to publicly state their position on breast versus bottle feeding. By 1958, the AAP published *Committee on Nutrition: On the Feeding of Solids to Infants.* This standard stressed the importance of breastfeeding for the infant, as well as established guidelines of proper nutrition for infants and children (AAP, 1958). The last 2 decades have seen numerous studies conducted exploring health outcomes of infants who were breastfed with those who were bottle fed. The results of these medical studies scientifically support the AAP publication of 1958 by showing that human-milk feeding protects against a variety of infant and childhood problems, such as otitis media, respiratory syncytial virus, and diarrheal diseases. This protection occurs primarily because of secretory IgA. Secretory IgA has demonstrated the ability to provide passive protection as well as provide a mechanism for active protection (AAP, 1997). Additional benefits for the infant include a possible link to greater cognitive development when a child is breastfed (Gale & Martyn, 1996).

Maternal benefits of breastfeeding include uterine involution and reduced risks of ovarian cancer and premenopausal breast cancer (AAP, 1997). Studies of mothers who breastfed their babies consistently reported mothers' feelings of greater closeness to the child and enjoyment of the "naturalness" of the breastfeeding process (AAP, 1997).

Economic benefits for the breastfed infant have been reported as well. Households who breastfeed experience the economic benefits, with savings estimated at $500 to $1000 per year (AAP, 1997). Breastfed infants have lower rates of acute and chronic illness than bottlefed infants, saving the national economy an expected 2.16 to 3.96 billion dollars annually (AAP, 1997).

Despite the benefits of breastfeeding, there are some medical situations where breastfeeding is not a benefit for the infant. These include the infants of mothers who have been infected with HIV, have untreated active tuberculosis, or use illicit drugs, and the infant who has been diagnosed with galactosemia (AAP, 1997).

INTRODUCTION OF SOLIDS DURING INFANCY

In the beginning of the 20th century, supplemental food was rarely offered until 1 year of age. By 1920, supplemental food offered to the infant consisted of cod liver oil to prevent rickets and orange juice to prevent scurvy (AAP, 1997). During the next 50 to 70 years, little cohesive medical advice existed concerning the optimal timing of solid food introduction. Through the 1940s and 1950s, the AAP remained a staunch advocate of breastfeeding as the optimal form of nutrition in the first year of life (AAP, 1997). Yet, the very group that reinforced "breast is best" was allowing conflicting information. By the 1950s and the 1960s, breastfeeding was encouraged, but accepting solid food at 1 week was considered a developmental milestone for the child (Weigley, 1990). No research at that time documented the support for early feeding of solids.

Since 1980, infant nutrition guidelines included breastfeeding or formula until at least 4 to 6 months, at which time solids were to be introduced (AAP, 1997). Essentially, the introduction of various foods was recommended to: (a) supply a more appealing, diversified diet for the infant; (b) supply energy, iron, and vitamins; and (c) provide needed trace elements (AAP, 1997). With these guidelines, what has now evolved is a relaxed approach to food introduction, with a general rule that it occur no earlier than 4 to 6 months of age. The decision to recommend the start of solids during this age period has been found to be based more on neuromuscular and developmental readiness of the child, rather than any hard scientific data. By 4 to 6 months, the infant gastrointestinal tract, though still maturing, is ready to digest and absorb proteins, fats, and carbohydrates. Kidney function has matured to the point of being able to excrete osmolar loads without the potential of excessive water loss (AAP, 1997; Oski, 1994). If the infant at 4 to 6 months has lost his or her extrusion reflex, can coordinate chewing and swallowing of nonliquid foods, and can sit up, the child is ready for solids (Suskind & Lewinter-Suskind, 1993). Timing of food introduction truly depends on developmental readiness of the infant. Not all 4-month-old infants are neurologically or developmentally ready for nonliquid foods.

Despite these well-publicized guidelines, it has been found that mothers will still go by personal or family opinion when introducing solids. One study showed that half of the mothers from middle/upper socioeconomic backgrounds introduced cereal well before the recommended 4 months of age. Cereal was typically added into the bottle of formula. This occurred even after anticipatory guidance was given at early well child visits (Skinner et al., 1997).

The AAP (1997) also states that "delay in introducing supplemental foods beyond 6 months may delay the timely appearance of other developmental milestones" (p. 52). No research has been found to support this statement. Even with recommended guidelines, parental decision is probably the greatest indicator of when an infant starts solids.

RELATIONSHIP OF FOOD INTRODUCTION AND THE DEVELOPMENT OF FOOD ALLERGY

There has only been one, well-documented reason to wait until 4 months to begin solid foods: formulation of food allergy. Atopic-prone infants have been shown through the literature to be at the highest risk for food allergies. Atopic dermatitis is multifactorial, with hypersensitivity developing through exposure to many allergens in the environment, possibly even in utero (Kjellman & Croner, 1984). In a hallmark study of 1,262 2-year-old children, Fergusson, Horwood, Beautrias, Shannon, and Taylor (1981) showed that children of atopic parents who received food before 4 months of age, had over 2-1/2 times the rate of eczema compared to children who were not fed earlier than 4 months and who were born to nonatopic parents. This study also demonstrated that the rate of eczema occurring was directly proportional to the different types of solids given (Fergusson et al., 1981). Further studies concluded that 72% of food allergies in infants were related to eggs, peanuts, and cow's milk.

Different studies have investigated the effect of breastfeeding on food allergy development. While it is known that the infant receives immunologic protection, it is also thought that there is exposure to potential allergens through human milk, which can result in subsequent sensitization to that specific allergen (Suskind & Lewinter-Suskind, 1993).

To prevent food allergies, soy formula is sometimes recommended for the child. Yet, studies evaluating the effectiveness of soy formula have mixed results; soy formulas cause hypersensitivity similar to that with milk proteins. Soy formula can also cause delayed hypersensitivity in infants who may be at risk for skin atopy, but it has not been shown to prevent allergy later in life (Suskind & Lewinter-Suskind, 1993). The recommendations for food introduction in allergy-prone infants appear to have been based on the concept of prevention, which suggests the elimination of major food allergens (i.e., peanuts, tree nuts, cow's milk, and eggs) from the infant and/or lactating mother. Prevention for the high risk infant includes: (a) maternal restrictions during pregnancy; (b) exclusive breastfeeding during the first 4 to 6 months with restrictions on peanuts, tree nuts, and possibly milk and eggs from the maternal diet; (c) hypoallergenic formula if breastfeeding is not possible; and

(d) reinforcing the delay of solid foods until after 4 to 6 months of age (AAP, 1997; Halken, Host, Hansen, & Osterballe, 1992; Zeiger et al., 1992). Following these guidelines appears to prevent some food allergy or atopic dermatitis. Also included in the list of foods for the child to avoid during the first year of life are fish, chocolate, and citrus (Oski, 1994), yet no studies have documented these as allergenic in children under 1 year of age, even those considered high risk for food allergy. Tradition again, not science, seems to dictate this recommendation.

SEQUENCING OF SOLID FOOD INTRODUCTION

The order of food introduction, as well as specific amounts to be given, are based on tradition rather than on scientific fact. No scientific studies have been performed to determine if there is a specific order of infant food introduction necessary or amounts needed for optimal development. The sequence of solids typically recommended by the AAP is cereal, fruits, vegetables, and meats (AAP, 1997). When introducing these foods, it has always been encouraged to wait 1 week between new foods to evaluate for food reactions. This waiting period is based on tradition, with no scientific basis.

The viewpoint of waiting between new foods has not changed, but the viewpoint of food sequencing has changed. Food should no longer be introduced in a rigid manner; each food should be introduced as the infant is ready. This is to be determined when the health care provider and the parent see age-appropriate growth, development, and activity (AAP, 1997).

When introducing solids into the diet of the infant, the caregiver needs to introduce single-ingredient foods on a weekly basis to monitor for food intolerance. A good choice as a first supplemental food is infant cereal. Cereal, such as rice cereal, provides additional energy and iron, contains no gluten, and is usually well tolerated.

When first feeding the infant solids, the AAP (1997) recommends mixing up to four tablespoons of rice cereal per day with breastmilk or formula. As the infant matures and tolerates solids, pureed vegetables, fruits, and meats can be added. The order of food introduction is not critical (AAP, 1997).

When solids are introduced at 4 to 6 months of age, the volume of formula or human milk may decrease. Breastfed infants, typically by the age of 9 months, will increase solid food intake and outgrow their supply of breastmilk. By the age of 10 to 12 months, formula fed infants should decrease their formula intake to an average of 16 to 20 ounces per day. In fact, no definitive upper limit of formula for infants under 1 year of age is given in the literature. Instead, most health care providers do agree that additional calories should come in the form of solid food if formula intake is greater than 32 ounces per day (Oski, 1994).

INTRODUCTION OF FRUIT JUICE

Along with introduction of solids is the question of fruit juice introduction. Many caregivers are confused as to when to introduce fruit juice, what type to give, and what quantity or dilution to use. The AAP (1997) states that "juices may be introduced when the infant can drink from a cup; while juices provide carbohydrates and vitamin C, they should not replace milk or infant formula" (p. 47).

Fruit juice has been the cause of much debate. Studies are conflicting, and more are necessary to determine the effect of fruit juice on the development of obesity, failure to thrive, and short stature. One study showed that excessive juice intake had been a contributing factor in cases of nonorganic failure to thrive due to chronic diarrhea in eight children 14 to 27 months (Smith & Lifshitz, 1994). The average juice intake per day for the infant should be less than five fluid ounces per day; however many children consume considerably more, resulting in only 50% of children meeting the Recommended Daily Allowance (RDA) for calcium (Dennison, 1996). Over 50% of children under 1 year of age consume apple juice as their primary source of the daily-required fruit servings (Dennison, 1996). Apple juice and pear juice have been documented to be responsible for carbohydrate malabsorption in infants and children because of higher amounts of fructose and sorbitol. These two fruit juices have been linked to gastrointestinal symptoms, such as diarrhea, tooth decay, failure to thrive, and obesity (Lifshitz, 1996).

What is clear in the literature is that white grape juice contains equimolar amounts of fructose and glucose, has no sorbitol, and is better absorbed by infants and children (Lifshitz, 1996). White grape juice, when incorporated into the diet of a child 1 year of age or younger (if drinking less than 5 ounces per day), can be a healthy source of fruit in the infant diet (Dennison, 1996).

IMPLICATIONS FOR PRACTICE

The pediatric nurse is commonly asked questions about infant nutrition. Whether during the postpartum period when nurses help new mothers learn to feed their children or the office visit for the well-child exam, the nurse can be an important proponent of healthy nutrition for the infant. As the caregiver begins the process of food introduction to his or her infant, questions arise such as "What food do I start with," "What do I do about breastfeeding or the bottle," and "When will my baby be ready for table food." The following are guidelines that can be incorporated as the nurse teaches the parent about infant nutrition:

Breast versus bottle. When the mother is deciding to breast or bottle feed, it is important for the pediatric nurse to support the mother's decision and review the known advantages and disadvantages of both. Most importantly, health care providers should review the long-lasting effects of breastfeeding on infant immunity. Riordan (1997) states that "health care providers hesitate to inform parents about the hazards of not breastfeeding because they do not want parents, especially the bottle feeding mothers, to feel guilty" (p. 96). Whether the mother chooses to breast or bottle feed, the pediatric nurse must be prepared to support either decision and understand how to assist the mother incorporate nonliquid foods into the diet.

Introduction of solids. What the literature has revealed about the incorporation of solids into the infant's diet is that it is art more than science. Other than scientific-based principles for initiation of foods in children at-risk for allergy, most solid food introduction appears to be based on the tradition of health care providers through this century. What may be helpful are feeding guidelines for children ages 0 to 12 months (see Table 1). These guidelines are based on neuromuscular and developmental readiness of the child. Anticipatory guidance is a must, especially to delay food introduction until at least 4 to 6 months of age. As discussed in the study by Skinner et al. (1997), parents will ultimately add food to an infant's diet based on personal or family opinion.

Safety is an issue of importance at any time, especially with the introduction of new foods. The pediatric nurse needs to teach the caregiver about the hazard of choking with any solid foods. For infants, foods such as hot dogs, nuts, grapes, raw carrots, popcorn, and round candies have been documented as known choking hazards and should not be introduced into the diet until later in childhood (AAP, 1997).

Introduction of fruit juice. Research needs to continue in this area, especially studies to evaluate the long-term effects of juice consumption on children younger than 1 year of age. The pediatric nurse can follow AAP guidelines and encourage the caregiver not to substitute milk with fruit juice, in order for the child to obtain the needed calcium for growth. Fruit juice should be limited to white grape juice to decrease potential sequelae. Also, it should be limited to less than 5 ounces per day for children under 1 year of age. Juice given from a cup will help limit the volume as well as prevent possible formation of dental caries.

Future considerations in pediatric nutrition. Currently, pediatric guidelines are being evaluated more closely in the attempt to further decrease the risk of chronic diseases, such as diabetes or hyperlipidemia, later in life. In order to build a foundation for better adult health, greater attention is being paid to the introduction of supplemental foods and diet during the first 2 years of life (Kleinman, Finberg, Klish, & Lauer, 1996). This continues to be an expanding area of research, as preventive measures in pediatric nutrition will continue to be implemented to improve the lifestyles of children as they grow to adulthood.

As we start the new millennium, the pediatric nurse needs to continually be aware of changes in pediatric nutrition and how much of our knowledge is based on tradition rather than science. We, as a group, can impact the pediatric population and their caregivers by reinforcing the need for a healthy, balanced diet that can successfully start in infancy.

Table 1. Recommended Introduction of Foods in the First Year of Life

Age of Infant	Breast or Formula: Amounts decrease as age increases	Solid Foods: Amounts increase as age increases
0–4 months	Feedings: 5–10 per day Formula: 22–32 oz/day	None 1/3–1/2 cup infant cereal/day 2–4 tbsp fruits/day 2–4 tbsp vegetables/day
4–6 months	Feedings: 4–5 per day Formula: 30–32 oz/day	1–2 tbsp meats/day Texture: semiliquid to puree 1/3–1/2 cup infant cereal/day 2–5 tbsp fruits/day 2–5 tbsp vegetables/day 2–4 tbsp meats/day
6–8 months	Feedings: 3–4 per day Formula: 24–28 oz/day	2–3 tbsp potato or pasta/day 2–4 oz yogurt/day Finger foods: teething biscuits Texture: puree to mashed 1/2–2/3 cup infant cereal/day 4–6 tbsp fruits/day 4–6 tbsp vegetables/day 2–4 tbsp meats/day
8–10 months	Feedings: 3–4 per day Formula: 20–24 oz/day	2–4 tbsp potato or pasta/day 4 oz yogurt/day Finger foods: teething biscuits Texture: mashed to soft chunks for finger feeding 1/2–2/3 cup infant cereal/day 6–8 tbsp fruits/day 6–8 tbsp vegetables/day 5–6 tbsp meats/day
10–12 months	Feedings: 3–4 per day Formula: 18–20 oz/day	2–4 tbsp potato or pasta/day 4–6 oz yogurt/day Finger Foods: teething biscuits or 1/2 slice bread Egg: start at 12 months Texture: soft finely chopped table foods

Fruit Juice

Age of Infant	Amounts increase as age increases
0–4 months	None
4–6 months	3–4 oz/day
6–8 months	4 oz/day
8–10 months	4 oz/day
10–12 months	4–5 oz/day

CRITICAL THINKING QUESTIONS

1. Briefly summarize how recommendations have changed from the early 1900s to today regarding infant nutrition. What factors do you think have contributed to those changes?
2. How do you think an expectant mother could or should use this information to make decisions regarding nutrition for her infant?
3. Is there anything not covered in this article that you think would be important to know about infant nutrition?

REFERENCES

American Academy of Pediatrics (AAP). (1958). Committee on nutrition: On the feeding of solid foods to infants. *Pediatrics,* 21, 685–692.

American Academy of Pediatrics (AAP). (1997). *Pediatric nutrition handbook* (4th ed.). Elk Grove Village, IL: American Academy of Pediatrics.

Dennison, B.A. (1996). Fruit juice consumption by infants and children: A review. *Journal of the American College of Nutrition,* 15(Suppl.), 4S–11S.

Fergusson, D.M., Horwood, L.J., Beautrias, A.L., Shannon, F.T., & Taylor, B. (1981). Eczema and infant diet. *Clinical Allergy,* 11, 325–331.

Gale, C.R., & Martyn, C.N. (1996). Breastfeeding, dummy use, and adult intelligence. *The Lancet,* 347, 1072–1075.

Halken, S., Host, A., Hansen, L.G., & Osterballe, O. (1992). Effect of an allergy prevention program on incidence of atopic symptoms in infancy: A prospective study of 159 'high risk' infants. *Allergy,* 47, 543–553.

Hammer, D., Bryson, S., & Agras, S. (1999). Development of feeding practices during the first five years of life. *Archives of Pediatric and Adolescent Medicine,* 153, 189–194.

Kjellman, N., & Croner, S. (1984). Cord blood IgE determination for allergy prediction - A follow-up to seven years of age in 1651 children. *Annals of Allergy,* 53, 167–171.

Kleinman, R.E., Finberg, L.F., Klish, W.J., & Lauer, R.N. (1996). Dietary guidelines for children: U.S. recommendations. *Journal of Nutrition,* 126 (4 Suppl.), 1028S–1030S.

Lifshitz, F. (1996). Weaning foods . . . The role of fruit juice in the diets of infants and children. *Journal of the American College of Nutrition,* 15(Suppl.), 1S–3S.

Oski, F. (Ed.). (1994). *Principles and practice of pediatrics* (2nd ed.). Philadelphia: J.B. Lippincott.

Owen, A.L., & Owen, G.M. (1997). *Journal of the American Dietetic Association,* 97, 777–782.

Riordan, J.M. (1997). The cost of not breastfeeding: A commentary. *Journal of Human Lactation,* 13, 93–97.

Skinner, J.D., Carruth, B.R., Houck, K., Moran, J., Coletta, F., Cotter, R., Ott, D., & McLeod, M. (1997). Transitions in infant feeding during the first year of life. *Journal of the American College of Nutrition,* 16, 209–215.

Smith, M.M., & Lifshitz, F. (1994). Excess fruit juice consumption as a contributing factor in nonorganic failure to thrive. *Pediatrics,* 93, 438–443.

Suskind, R.M., & Lewinter-Suskind, L. (Eds.). (1993). *Textbook of pediatric nutrition* (2nd ed.). New York: Raven Press.

United States Public Health Service (USPHS). (1999). Healthy People 2000: Progress Review Maternal and Infant Health. [On-Line]. Available: http://odhhp.osoph.dhhs.gov/pubs/hp2000/prog_rvw/matinf99.pdf

Weigley, E.S. (1990). Changing patterns in offering solids to infants. *Pediatric Nursing,* 16, 439–441.

Zeiger, R.S., Heller, S., Mellon, M.H., Halsey, J.E, Hamburger, R.N., & Sampson, H.A. (1992). Genetic and environmental factors affecting development of atopy through age 4 in children of atopic parents: A prospective randomized study of food allergen avoidance. Pediatric *Allergy and Immunology,* 3, 110–127.

Christina J. Calamaro, MSN, CRNP, CPNP, is Clinical Coordinator, Graduate Nursing Programs, University of Delaware, Newark, DE.

6

Infancy: Cognitive Development

Responding to Joint Attention and Language Development: A Comparison of Target Locations

Christine E. F. Delgado, Peter Mundy, Mary Crowson,
Jessica Markus, Marygrace Yale, and Heidi Schwartz

This study examined the importance of target location (within vs. outside the visual field) on the relation between responding to joint attention and subsequent language development in 47 normally developing infants. The results supported a developmental progression in the infants' ability to locate targets from within to outside the visual field. In addition, individual differences in 15-month-old infants' ability to correctly locate targets outside the visual field was a unique predictor of expressive language at 24 months. Infants' ability to locate targets outside the visual field may demonstrate increasing capacities for attention regulation, representational thinking, and social cognition that may facilitate language learning. The implications of this study are discussed with regard to the usefulness of measures of responding to joint attention for identifying early language and developmental delays.

Journal of Speech, Language, and Hearing Research, August 2002, v45, i4, p715(5).

© 2002 American Speech-Language-Hearing Association.

The ability of infants to respond to joint attention, or to follow the visual regard of others, may reflect the development of important social, cognitive, and self-regulatory skills associated with the capacity to acquire language (Baldwin & Baird, 1999; Bates, 1979; Bruner, 1977; Moore & Corkum, 1994; Tomasello, 1988, 1995). In fact, several studies have indicated that individual differences in the ability of 6- to 18-month-old infants to respond to joint attention are predictive of language ability at 24 to 36 months (Markus, Mundy, Morales, Delgado, & Yale, 2000; Morales, Mundy, & Rojas, 1998; Mundy & Gomes, 1998; Mundy, Kasari, Sigman, & Ruskin, 1995). These studies, however, used scores of responding to joint attention that did not take target location into account. Infant responses to targets both within the visual field (90° or less to the left or right of the infant) and outside the visual field (> 90° to the left or right of the infant) were combined to predict later language development.

Developmental changes in the ability of infants to locate objects outside their visual field implicate target location as an important consideration that may reflect cognitive and social advances important to later language development. The ability of infants to locate the focus of another person's attention follows a predictable developmental path. Before 12 months, responding to joint attention is typically limited to targets within the infant's visual field. Between the ages of 12 and 18 months, infants develop the capacity to locate targets that are outside their visual field or behind them (Butterworth & Cochran, 1980; Butterworth & Jarrett, 1991). This developmental advancement is hypothesized to reflect improvement in the infant's spatial skills as well as the consolidation of social cognitive processes that enable infants to understand the implications of social gaze shifts and gestures. Specifically, for infants older than 12 months, individual differences in the developmentally more advanced task of locating targets outside the visual field may be a stronger predictor of language development than the task of locating targets within the visual field, which emerges at an earlier age.

METHOD

Participants

Forty-seven healthy, full-term infants (22 boys, 25 girls) were assessed. The infants were participants in a broader longitudinal study of infant social development. Information collected at the 15- and 24-month sessions was included in this study. All families were classified as middle or high socioeconomic status based on a synthesis of the SES evaluations of Hollingshead (1978) and Nam and Powers (1983) as adapted by Eilers et al. (1993). Twenty-one of the subjects were classified as White Non-Hispanic, 19 were Hispanic, 4 were African American, 2 were Asian, and 1 was classified as Other with respect to racial/ethnic background.

Procedure

All assessments were conducted in a university-based child laboratory. Responding to joint attention (RJA) was evaluated at 15 months of age using the Early Social Communication Scales (ESCS; Mundy, Hogan, & Doehring, 1996). During the ESCS, two sets of four pointing trials were administered in which the experimenter attempted to direct the infant's attention (by looking and pointing) to pictures of four cartoon characters placed on the walls to the infant's left, right, left behind, and right behind. The pictures were brightly colored representations of Disney cartoon characters and were approximately 11 inches long and 9 inches wide (some variations in size occurred because of the shape of the individual character). The characters were placed at approximately 60° (left/right) and 150° (left behind/right behind) from the infant's midline (see Figure 1). (All figures referenced can be found within the online version of this article, at http://www.infotrac-college.com.) The percent of trials in which the infant correctly turned his or her head in the direction of the tester's point was calculated for the combined Left and Right trials and for the combined Behind trials. For the Left/Right trials, the direction of the infant's gaze needed to shift beyond the tester's extended finger (approximately 45° off midline) to receive credit for the look. For the Behind trials, the infant needed to turn his or her head more than 90° off midline. All trials were coded from videotape by one individual who was blind to the infants' language and cognitive scores. An additional coder rated the trials of 9 of the infants to establish reliability. Reliability was determined based on agreement of pass/fail for each trial. The two coders demonstrated 94% agreement. Any procedural error observed by the coder resulted in the elimination of that RJA trial from all analyses. Ninety-five percent of all RJA trials were administered properly.

Language ability was assessed at 24 months of age using the Reynell Developmental Language Scales (RDLS; Reynell & Gruber, 1990). The infant's receptive language score was equal to the number of items passed on the Verbal Comprehension scale. The infant's expressive language score was calculated as the sum of the scores for the Structure and Vocabulary scales.

In addition, the general cognitive level of the infants was estimated at 15 months using the Bayley Scales of Infant Development-II (BSID-II, Bayley, 1993). Administration and scoring of items were performed in a standardized fashion, yielding an index score for cognitive development. The testers who administered and scored the RDLS and the BSID-II were unaware of the child's RJA score.

Results

Descriptive information for ILIA, language, and cognitive ability are presented in Table 1. Infants responded correctly on the Left/Right trials (M = 84.0%) to a significantly greater extent than they did on the Behind trials (M = 39.4%)

Table 1. Descriptive Information for Responding to Joint Attention, Cognitive Ability, Receptive and Expressive Language

MEASURES	M	SD	MIN	MAX
ESCS-RJA (a) (15 months)				
Left/Right Trials (% correct)	84.04	22.38	25.00	100.00
Behind Trials (% correct)	39.43	39.61	0.00	100.00
Total (% correct)	62.35	25.90	12.50	100.00
BSID-II (b) (15 months)				
MDI (c)	101.72	9.00	83	117
RDLS (d) (24 months)				
Receptive Language (total score)	20.57	8.02	3	34
Expressive Language (total score)	23.36	5.16	12	32

Note: N = 47
(a) Early Social Communication Scales-Responding to Joint Attention measure
(b) Bayley Scales of Infant Development-II
(c) Mental Development Index
(d) Reynell Developmental Language Scales

[$t(46) = 8.23$, $p < .01$]. In fact, 45 out of the 47 infants scored 50% or better on Left/Right trials, whereas only 18 of the infants scored 50% or better on Behind trials. In addition, scores of receptive and expressive language were found to be significantly correlated [$r(46) = .55$, $p < .01$]. Because of the moderate size of the correlation, receptive and expressive language were considered to be related, but not orthogonal, variables and were evaluated independently rather than by combining them into a composite language score.

Hierarchical linear regression analyses indicated that performance on the combination of Left/Right and Behind trials significantly predicted expressive language score ($R^2 = .30$, $p < .01$), but only marginally predicted receptive language score ($R^2 = .11$, $p = .09$). Although performance on the Left/Right and Behind trials was significantly correlated [$r(46) = .39$, $p < .01$], when performance on the Left/Right trials was controlled for, infant performance on the Behind trials explained unique variance in expressive language ($B = .07$, $p < .01$; see Table 2). Expressed in terms of partial correlation, percent correct on Behind trials remained significantly correlated with expressive language even after considering the variance associated with accuracy on Left/Right trials [$\partial - r(44) = .49$, $p < .01$].

With regard to receptive language, the ability of performance on the Behind trials to uniquely predict variance in language over and above the Left/Right trials only approached conventional significance levels ($B = .06$, $p = .06$; see Table 2). The correlation of percent correct on Behind trials with receptive language approached conventional levels of significance when the variance

Table 2. Hierarchical Regression Analysis Summary for RJA Trials Predicting Language

	EXPRESSIVE LANGUAGE	
F	**Adj. R^2**	**B**
Step 1	18.82**	.28
Behind Trials		.07**
Step 2	9.40**	.27
Behind Trials		.07**
Left/Right Trials		.02
	RECEPTIVE LANGUAGE	
F	**Adj. R^2**	**B**
Step 1	5.17*	.08
Behind Trials		0.7*
Step 2	2.61†	.07
Behind Trials		.06†
Left/Right Trials		.02

Note: All reported significance levels are two-tailed.
*p < .05
**p < .01
†p < .10

associated with accuracy on Left/Right trials was considered [∂ − r(44) = .28, p = .06].

The examination of the general cognitive ability of the infants provides a source of incremental validity with regard to the relations between the RJA Behind trials and later language ability. The mental development index (MDI) score calculated from the administration of the BSID-II at 15 months was significantly correlated with the concurrent measures of RJA for Behind trials [r(46) = .41, p < .01] but not for Left/Right trials [r(46) = .19, p = .19]. MDI scores at 15 months were also significantly correlated with both expressive and receptive language scores on the RDLS at 24 months [r(46) = .49, p < .01 and r(46) = .34, p = .02, respectively]. The percent correct on Behind trials remained significantly correlated with expressive language even after considering the variance associated with the general cognitive ability (MDI) [∂ − r(44) = .43, p < .01]. Therefore, infants who identified more targets outside their visual field at 15 months tended to have higher expressive language scores at 24 months, independent of their general cognitive level. For receptive language, however, percent correct on Behind trials was not significantly correlated with receptive language when the variance associated with general cognitive ability (MDI) was controlled for [∂ − r(44) = .21, p = .15].

DISCUSSION

These results are consistent with the previously established notion of a developmental progression in infants' ability to locate targets from within the visual field to targets located outside the visual field (Butterworth & Cochran, 1980; Butterworth & Jarrett, 1991). The 15-month-old infants in this study appeared to be quite capable of locating targets within their visual field. Fewer of the infants, however, displayed a consistent ability to locate targets outside their visual field.

Individual differences in the ability of these normally developing infants to locate targets outside their visual field were shown to provide unique information about developing expressive language skills. Success on Behind trials at 15 months may reflect individual differences in the maturation of the social-cognitive abilities that facilitate language learning. For infants to be able to use social information such as gaze direction and pointing to locate an object outside the visual field requires increasingly mature spatial skills, an understanding of the intent of the communicative partner, and the cognitive ability to determine the precise location of the object relative to the body. The increasing capacity to locate an object that is being labeled or described maximizes the opportunity for forming accurate word-object matchings, as well as for increasing the capacity to gain from a wider variety of learning situations. In addition, it is quite possible that infants' ability to monitor direction of gaze within the visual field becomes routinized during the 12 to 18 month period. If so, this may allow the infant to use gaze-following to decrease referential mapping errors (Baldwin, 1995) and to devote increasing amounts of mental capacity to linguistic processing in incidental referential learning situations.

The relation of responding to joint attention with language was not consistent across the receptive and expressive language measures, with significant relations found only for the expressive language measures. Several previous studies have reported significant correlations of responding to joint attention with both receptive and expressive language (Morales et al., 1998; Mundy & Gomes, 1998; Mundy et al., 1995). At least one prior study, however, has reported that responding to joint attention was significantly correlated with expressive, but not receptive, language (Markus et al., 2000). It is important to note, however, that early expressive vocabulary may be more reliably assessed than receptive vocabulary in general (Bates, Bretherton, & Snyder, 1998) and specifically with the RDLS (Reynell & Gruber, 1990).

The presence of ceiling effects for the Left/Right trials represents a limitation of the present study. Infants in the present study were observed at 15 months of age in an attempt to maximize variability in gaze-following for the Behind trials. Because of the developmental changes associated with the ability to respond to joint attention tasks (Butterworth & Cochran, 1980; Butterworth & Jarrett, 1991), the infants observed were quite capable of locating a target within their visual field, resulting in reduced variability for the Left/Right trials. Although this limits the ability to examine the relation between Left/Right trials and language development, the findings with regard to the Behind trials raise the issue that the relation between responding to joint attention and language development is likely based on the child's developmental level. This finding is particularly important for establishing the clinical utility of the responding-to-joint-attention trials. Clinically and developmentally, overall performance on a set of responding-to-joint-attention trials may not be as informative as performance based on the location of the targets. Future research is necessary to develop a more complete picture of the developmental influences on the relations between responding to joint attention and language development.

In summary, the results of the present study verify that target location is an important consideration when studying the relation between the ability of infants to respond to joint attention and their subsequent language development. These findings also have implications for the use of measures of nonverbal communication, particularly responding to joint attention, in infant assessment tools. Responding to joint attention is an efficiently and reliably indexed aspect of infant social cognition that appears to have incremental validity with regard to the prediction of individual differences in early vocabulary development. As such, it may be useful to incorporate measures of responding to joint attention in clinical infant assessment batteries. Before this step can be taken in an optimally effective fashion, however, it will be necessary to have a clear picture of the developmental progression of different aspects of joint attention. It will also likely be necessary to develop an understanding of the window of maximal developmental sensitivity for different types of joint attention measures, as these are likely to vary across the first two years of life. This study provides an illustrative initial step for research of this kind.

ACKNOWLEDGMENTS

This study was part of a program of research supported by a grant from the National Institute of Deafness and Other Communication Disorders (DC00484). The authors would like to thank the families involved in this project for their gracious participation.

CRITICAL THINKING QUESTIONS

1. In your own words briefly summarize this research including design and results. What do you think are the most important findings in this research?
2. What implications do you think this research might have in terms of interventions for caregivers and infants?
3. Do you think there are any biases in this research? If so what are they and how would you correct for them?

REFERENCES

Baldwin, D. A. (1995). Understanding the link between joint attention and language. In C. Moore & P. J. Dunham (Eds.), *Joint attention: Its origins and role in development* (pp. 131–158). Hillsdale, NJ: Lawrence Erlbaum.

Baldwin, D. A., & Baird, J. A. (1999). Action analysis: A gateway to intentional inference. In P. Rochat (Ed.), *Early social cognition: Understanding others in the first months of life* (pp. 215–240). Mahwah, NJ: Lawrence Erlbaum.

Bates, E. (1979). *The emergence of symbols: Cognition and communication in infancy.* New York: Academic Press.

Bates, E., Bretherton, I., & Snyder, L. (1988). *From first words to grammar: Individual differences and dissociable mechanisms.* New York: Cambridge University Press.

Bayley, N. (1993). *Barley Scales of Infant Development* (2nd ed.). San Antonio: Psychological Corp.

Bruner, J. S. (1977). Early social interaction and language acquisition. In H. R. Schaffer (Ed.), *Studies in mother-infant interaction* (pp. 271–289). London: Academic Press.

Butterworth, G. E., & Cochran, E. (1980). Towards a mechanism of joint visual attention in human infancy. *International Journal of Behavioural Development,* 3, 253–272.

Butterworth, G., & Jarrett, N. (1991). What minds have in common is space: Spatial mechanisms serving joint visual attention in infancy. *British Journal of Developmental Psychology,* 9, 55–72.

Eilers, R. E., Oiler, D. K., Levine, S., Basinger, D., Lynch, M. P., & Urbano, R. (1993). The role of prematurity and socioeconomic status in the onset of canonical babbling in infants. *Infant Behavior and Development,* 16, 297–315.

Hollingshead, A. B. (1978). *Two-factor index of social status.* New Haven, CT: Yale University Press.

Markus, J., Mundy, P., Morales, M., Delgado, C. E. F., & Yale, M. (2000). Individual differences in infant skill as predictors of child-caregiver joint attention and language. *Social Development,* 9, 302–315.

Moore, C., & Corkum, V. (1994). Social understanding at the end of the first year of life. *Developmental Review,* 14, 349–372.

Morales, M., Mundy, P., & Rojas, J. (1998). Gaze following and language development in six-month-olds. *Infant Behavior and Development,* 21, 373–377.

Mundy, P., Card, J., & Fox, N. (2000). EEG correlates of the development of infant joint attention skills. *Developmental Psychobiology,* 36, 325–338.

Mundy, P., & Gomes, A. (1998). Individual differences in joint attention skill development in the second year. *Infant Behavior and Development,* 21, 469–482.

Mundy, P., Hogan, A., & Doehring, P. (1996). A preliminary manual for the abridged Early Social Communication Scales (ESCS). Retrieved December 10, 2001, from University of Miami-Coral Gables, Psychology Department Web site: http://www.psy.miami.edu/child/pmundy

Mundy, P., Kasari, C., Sigman, M., & Ruskin, E. (1995). Nonverbal communication and early language acquisition in children with Down syndrome and in normally developing children. *Journal of Speech and Hearing Research,* 38, 157–167.

Nam, C. V., & Powers, N. G. (1983). *Socioeconomic approach to status measurement.* Houston, TX: Cap & Gown Press.

Reynell, J., & Gruber, C. (1990). *Reynell Developmental Language Scales: US edition.* Los Angeles: Western Psychological Services.

Tomasello, M. (1988). The role of joint attention in early language development. *Language Sciences,* 11, 69–88.

Tomasello, M. (1995). Joint attention as social cognition. In C. Moore & P. Dunham (Eds.), *Joint attention: Its origins and role in development* (pp. 103–130). Hillsdale, NJ: Lawrence Earlbaum.

7

Infancy: Social and Emotional Development

Understanding Child Temperament Can Have Far-Reaching Impact on Behavior and Quality of Life

Barbara K. Keogh

Children bring a wide range of personal characteristics to their daily lives. They differ in cognitive aptitudes, in language facility, in motivation, even in physical size and appearance. They also differ in temperament, a less well-studied dimension of individual differences, but one which affects their experiences at home and at school.

We all know people who have a slow tempo, who move at an unhurried pace, who are slow to respond and slow to action. We also know highly active, intense, quick reacting people who go through life at high speed. We recognize that some children are uncomfortable with change and are shy with new people, while others thrive on novelty, seek out new experiences and interact quickly with those around them. These characteristics are expressions of temperament.

The Brown University Child and Adolescent Behavior Letter, Oct 2003, v19, i10, p1(3).

© 2003 Manisses Communications Group, Inc. Reprinted with permission.

Children obviously are affected by the environments in which they live, but environmental conditions do not operate on a tabula rosa or blank slate, and temperament is one of the individual differences that make children unique and which contribute to their development, behavior and adjustment.

WHAT IS TEMPERAMENT?

There are a number of specific definitions of temperament, but there is overall agreement that temperament is biologically based, is evident early in life and has some stability over time and situations. Think of the differences in how two 6-month old infants react to a sudden loud noise. One is startled, distressed, agitated and cries vigorously; the other turns his head slowly and looks with interest to find the source of the noise. Think of the quick responding, highly reactive and intense adolescent with a "short fuse" or the adolescent who is quiet, reflective and deliberate.

One of the most widely accepted and clinically useful definitions of temperament is that of psychiatrists Thomas and Chess (1977) who described temperament as behavioral style. In their view, temperament is the how of behavior. It differs from ability, which is the "what and how well" of behavior, and from motivation, which refers to "why" an individual chooses to do what he does. Thomas and Chess identified nine dimensions of temperament: 1) activity level; 2) rhythmicity; 3) approach/withdrawal; 4) adaptability; 5) threshold of responsiveness; 6) intensity of reaction; 7) quality of mood; 8) distractibility; 9) attention span/persistence.

Based on these nine dimensions, Thomas and Chess described three major types of temperamentally different children. "Easy" children are characteristically adaptable, positive in mood and moderate in the intensity of their reactions. They are interested and approaching to novelty and are sociable and friendly. "Difficult" children, in contrast, tend to be negative in mood, intense, low in adaptability and withdrawing in new situations. They are sometimes described as "prickly." A third group, those considered "slow-to-warm-up," differs from both easy and difficult peers. While initially shy and withdrawing in new situations they are moderate in the intensity of their reactions, but given time they adapt well and when comfortable, they are positive in mood, responsive and sociable. It should come as no surprise that parents and teachers find life more pleasant with easy children than with those considered difficult, and that slow to warm up children may require especially sensitive responses from adults.

WHY IS TEMPERAMENT IMPORTANT?

Temperament is important for several reasons. It describes individual behavioral styles that contribute to personal/social interactions, it evokes responses from others in the child's life and it affects the range and nature of children's experiences. An approaching, friendly and active child is likely to seek out new situations, whereas a withdrawing, timid child will avoid them. As a consequence, some children have a broader range of experiences than do others. Indeed, it is even possible that high energy, active children may sometimes put themselves in risky situations that are never experienced by their more withdrawing and less energetic peers.

Developmental psychologists stress that adult-child interactions are reciprocal—that is, that adults influence children's behavior, but that children also influence adults' behavior. Parents of highly active, intense, "fearless" toddlers may have to make special arrangements in their home to ensure a child's safety and teachers may have to give special attention to slow-to-warm-up students who tend to be overlooked in busy classrooms.

Children also evoke different affective responses from others around them, in part based on their temperaments. Children with difficult temperaments are more apt to elicit negative, even punitive, reactions from parents and teachers than are those with easy temperaments. This leads to the notion of "goodness of fit" which is central in understanding how temperament contributes to children's development and experiences.

Goodness of Fit

Goodness of fit refers to the match between a child's characteristics and the characteristics of the environment—including the values, expectations, demands and temperaments of adults. A child's behavioral style may fit well with parents' expectations and the daily routines in a family, or may have an intrusive or disruptive effect. Similarly, a child's temperament may or may not fit well with classroom demands. Classrooms, like families, are complex social settings with both explicit and implicit rules and expectations for children's behavior. Classrooms differ, some being highly structured, even rigid, others being free flowing, sometimes chaotic.

How children respond to these differences in part relates to the individual differences in temperament they bring to the classroom. For example, slow-to-warm-up children may not do well in fast-paced instructional programs and may be overwhelmed in free flowing "open" classrooms where there is a high level of activity and where routines change daily, even hourly. Intense, active and impulsive children may have problems in classrooms with rigidly defined rules and work periods that demand persistence and quiet concentration over long periods of time. It is important to note that teachers, too, differ in temperament—some being highly active, intense and impulsive, others being slow in tempo, slow-to-warm-up and shy. Fast paced teachers may see shy and withdrawing children as unresponsive and unmotivated, while more reticent, slow-to-warm-up teachers may see the behavior of high energy and intense children as troublesome.

HOW CAN AWARENESS OF TEMPERAMENT BE USEFUL?

Recognizing individual differences in temperament can help parents and teachers in several ways. First, it broadens adults' views about children's behavior, especially adults' views about problem behaviors. Adults frequently attribute motivational reasons for troublesome behaviors, as for example, "He could do it if only he would try harder" or "She just refuses to try anything new."

Being aware of individual differences in temperament helps parents and teachers reframe their ideas about the reasons for particular behaviors and leads to considering problems in a different context. The result is reduced negative affect and frustration and improved interactions.

Second, and closely linked, awareness of differences in temperament can help parents and teachers anticipate potential problem situations. Waiting in line for long periods of time is an invitation for trouble in a group of active 9-year-old boys. Slow-to-warm-up children may have difficulty getting started when faced with new tasks and new demands and need to be alerted to upcoming changes in home or classroom routines. Finally sensitivity to temperamental differences points directions for intervention.

Forewarned is forearmed and many problems can be prevented of minimized by considering the behavioral styles of the children relative to the expectations and demands of the situation. Minor modifications in daily routines can often improve the goodness of fit between child and setting and thus reduce tensions and negative feelings.

In summary, temperament researchers have documented that there are real individual differences in children's temperaments or behavioral styles which affect their everyday lives and experiences and their relationships with others. The role of temperament is best understood within an interactional framework in which the characteristics of both children and adults are important. Temperament is part of the goodness of fit between child and environment.

CRITICAL THINKING QUESTIONS

1. What are the nine dimensions Thomas and Chess used to classify temperament? Give an example of each of these. Are there any other dimensions you would include in this list? Why?
2. How do you think teachers could use this information to better understand and work with their students? Give some examples of how this information could help guide instruction in a classroom.
3. How do you think parents could use this information to better understand their children? How could they apply this to how they approach discipline with their children? Give some specific examples.

4. Which of the temperament patterns best describes you? Has your temperament pattern been consistent throughout your lifespan or have there been changes over the years? What might account for this stability or this change?

REFERENCES

Carey WB, McDevitt SC: *Coping with Children's Temperament.* New York: Basic Books, 1995.

Thomas A, Chess S: *Temperament and Development.* New York: Brunner/Mazel, 1977.

8

Early Childhood: Physical Development

Television and Food Advertising: An International Health Threat to Children?

Mary Story

Obesity is now considered one of the primary child health problems in industrialised countries (1, 2). Over the past few decades, obesity rates have increased two to threefold in most developed countries (1, 2). As a result of these trends, rates of type 2 diabetes are increasing in youth (3). Studies have also shown that 60% of overweight children have at least one cardiovascular disease risk factor (4). Left unabated obesity may eventually cause as much preventable disease and death as cigarette smoking (5). To ameliorate obesity during childhood, improvements are needed in the dual areas of physical activity and eating behaviours. It is widely agreed that increases in obesity prevalence are related, in part, to changes in the environment that encourage a positive energy balance. These include increases in the availability and marketing of food products, and increased time spent in sedentary activities (6). Thus, macro level influences on obesity risk must be considered in developing interventions to

Nutrition & Dietetics: The Journal of the Dieticians Association of Australia, June 2003, v60, i2, p72(2).

© 2003 Dietitians Association of Australia. Reprinted with permission.

improve weight outcomes. One macro level influence that impacts both eating behaviour and physical activity is the media. Television has been cited as a contributing factor to higher energy intakes (6). Two possible mechanisms have been proposed linking television viewing and obesity:

(1) reduced energy expenditure from excessive television viewing displacing physical activity; and

(2) increased dietary energy intake from eating during viewing or from food advertising (7).

Children view an average of almost three hours of television per day (8, 9). Since television is the most widely used advertising medium, it is important to examine exposure to food messages. The study in this issue by Zuppa, Morton and Mehta is important because it documents the types of foods advertised during programs that appeal to children. They found that of the 63 hours of television taped, there were 544 food advertisements; 79% were for non-core foods of the Australian Guide to Healthy Eating. Almost half of the food advertisements were for fast foods and confectionery. Based on this data, children are exposed to one food advertisement on television every seven minutes, and the foods advertised disproportionately promote the consumption of foods high in fat, energy and sugar. As stated in the article by Zuppa and colleagues, Australian children watch an average of 23 hours of television a week. Thus, Australian children are exposed to over 10,000 food advertisements every year. Other content analyses studies (9–12) have shown results similar to the study by Zuppa et al. The majority of studies show that television food advertisements on children's programming target highly sweetened products, and the proportion of advertisements from fast food restaurants is increasing. The study by Zuppa and colleagues, together with other studies, clearly shows that this is an international issue.

Children are being exposed to an increasing and unprecedented barrage of advertisements (13), The principal goal of commercial children's television is to sell products to children, with food and toys being the two most frequently advertised product categories (8). The heavy marketing of high fat foods and food of low nutritional value targetted to children can be viewed as exploitation because young children do not understand that commercials are designed to sell products and do not have the cognitive ability to comprehend or evaluate advertising (8). Numerous studies have documented that children under eight years of age are developmentally unable to understand the intent of advertisements (8, 13).

We know that the foods advertised on television are targetted to children across several countries and predominantly for products high in fat, sugar, salt and that these foods are inconsistent with recommendations for good health. However, a critical issue is whether exposure to these food advertisements have any observable effects on children's dietary intake, eating behaviour and weight status. One problem in assessing the impact of television food advertisements is that food advertisements and television are both pervasive and distal, and it is difficult to conduct studies to distinguish effects from confounding variables. Compared to content analyses studies, there have been fewer studies on actual eating behaviour, and most of these studies were conducted in the 1970s and 1980s. The majority of correlational and experimental studies have shown that the amount of time spent viewing television directly correlates with children's food requests, preferences, purchase and consumption of foods advertised on te levision. For example, Taras et al. (14) interviewed 66 mothers of children aged three to eight years, to assess children's viewing habits and children's requests for food advertised on television. The foods that children requested most frequently because they had seen them on television were the foods most frequently advertised on television. Weekly viewing hours correlated significantly with:

(1) reported number of requests by children, and purchases by parents of foods advertised on television; and
(2) children's energy intake; children who watched more television consumed more calories.

These results were similar to those of Galst and White (15) who observed child–mother interaction in the supermarket and then interviewed mothers on their child's television viewing habits. They found that children's television viewing hours correlated with consumption of foods advertised on television and children's attempts to influence their mother's food purchases.

Controlled experimental studies with children have also demonstrated direct effects of exposure to advertising for high energy foods and snack-food choices and consumption. To date, no studies have shown the effect of television food advertising on actual weight status. Increasing amounts of time watching television has been associated with higher intakes of energy, fat, sweet and salty snacks, and carbonated beverages, and lower intakes of fruit and beverages (11). In addition, several large studies have documented associations between number of hours of television watched and the prevalence and incidence of obesity (11). We need the next generation of studies to delve into exposure to television food advertisements and impact on obesity risk and overall dietary intake patterns.

It is evident from the study by Zuppa et al., as well as other studies (9-12), that food advertisements aimed at young children attempt to persuade them to adopt eating patterns contrary to the principles of healthy eating. This is an important public health issue that warrants an international dialogue to discuss ethical concerns and social responsibility towards children, as well as policy, advocacy and education issues and actions to ensure that messages reaching children are in their best interests.

Mary Story, PhD, RD, is Professor, Division of Epidemiology and Associate Dean for Student Affairs School of Public Health University of Minnesota Minneapolis, USA.

CRITICAL THINKING QUESTIONS

1. What facts does this author present that would support the hypothesis that television and food advertising are an international health threat? Is there adequate support given in this article to prove this hypothesis?
2. What are the two proposed mechanisms linked to television watching and childhood obesity? Do you agree with these two? Are there others you would propose?
3. This information presented in this article is primarily from Australia. In what ways do you think this information would generalize to children in other parts of the world? In what ways would it not?
4. Both correlational and experimental research is presented in this article. What are the major differences in these two types of research and how do you think each helps support or refute the hypothesis?

REFERENCES

1. Ebbeling C, Pawlak D, Ludwig D. Childhood obesity: public-health crisis, common sense cure. *Lancet* 2002;360:473.
2. World Health Organization. *The World Health Report 2002. Reducing Risks, Promoting Healthy Life.* Geneva: WHO; 2002.
3. American Diabetes Association. Type 2 diabetes in children and adolescents. *Pediatrics* 2000;105:671–80.
4. Freedman DS, Dietz WH, Srinivasan SR, Berenson GS. The relation of overweight to cardiovascular risk factors among children and adolescents: the Bogalusa Heart Study. *Pediatrics* 1999;103:1175–82.
5. US Department of Health and Human Services. *The Surgeon General's call to action to prevent and decrease overweight and obesity.* Rockville, MD: US Department of Health and Human Services, Public Health Service, Office of the Surgeon General: 2001.
6. French SA, Story M, Jeffery RW. Environmental influences on eating and physical activity. *Annu Rev Public Health* 2001;22:309–35.
7. Robinson TN. Television viewing and childhood obesity. *Pediatr Clin North Am* 2001;48:1017–25.
8. American Academy of Pediatrics. Children, adolescents, and advertising. Committee on Communications, American Academy of Pediatrics. *Pediatrics* 1995;95:295–7.
9. Consumers International. *A spoonful of sugar. Television food advertising aimed at children: an international comparative study.* London: Consumers International; 1996.

10. Kitz K, Story M. Food advertisements during children's Saturday morning television programming: Are they consistent with dietary recommendations? *J Am Diet Assoc* 1994;94:1296–300.

11. Coon KA, Tucker KL. Television and children's consumption patterns. A review of the literature. *Minerva Pediatr* 2002;54:423–36.

12. Sustain: The Alliance for Better Food and Farming. *TV Dinners: What's being served up by the advertisers.* London: Sustain: The Alliance for Better Food and Farming; 2001. p. 1–31.

13. Strasburger VC. Children and TV advertising: nowhere to run, nowhere to hide. *J Dev Behav Pediatr* 2001;22:185–7.

14. Taras HL, Sallis JF, Patterson TL, Nader PR, Nelson JA. Television's influence on children's diet and physical activity. *J Dev Behav Pediatr* 1989;10:176–80.

15. Galst J, White M. The unhealthy persuader: the reinforcing value of television and children's purchase—influencing attempts at the supermarket. *Child Development* 1976;47:1089–96.

9

Early Childhood: Cognitive Development

Characteristics of Preschool and School-Age Children with Imaginary Companions

Paula Bouldin and Chris Pratt

The authors investigated the prevalence and characteristics of children who experience or who have experienced imaginary companions. For the study, a self-administered questionnaire that sought information regarding the characteristics of children with and without imaginary companions was completed by 478 parents of children within the age range of 3 to 9.5 years. A significantly larger number of children with imaginary companions were reported to be first-born children, to be very imaginative, to incorporate myth in their play, and to explain events as magical. Overall, these results are interpreted to indicate that birth order, combined with characteristics such as imaginativeness and a predisposition to engage in fantasy, characterizes children with imaginary companions.

Both anecdotal reports and research evidence suggest that many children have imaginary companions during the preschool years (e.g., Fraiberg, 1968; Mauro, 1990; D. G. Singer & Singer, 1990). These companions may take the form of humans, animals, toys, or television characters, and children

Journal of Genetic Psychology, Dec 1999, v160, i4, p397(1).

© 1999 Heldref Publications.

often include them in their daily routines (Jalongo, 1984; Jersild, 1968; D. G. Singer & Singer, 1990; Somers & Yawkey, 1984).

However, although the positive effects of these companions on children's emotional and cognitive development have been reported repeatedly in the literature (e.g., Ames & Learned, 1946; Mauro, 1990; J. L. Singer, 1961; J. L. Singer & Singer, 1981), many of the methodologies used, in early studies in particular, have been questionable (e.g., Ames & Learned, 1946; Jersild, Markey, & Jersild, 1933; Vostrovsky, 1895).

This concern was addressed by Manosevitz, Prentice, and Wilson (1973), who conducted one of the most systematic investigations of the factors associated with the presence or absence of imaginary companions. Parents of preschool children were administered a self-report questionnaire that requested information on factors such as their child's birth order, play activities, and personality characteristics. The results indicated that birth order was associated with the presence of imaginary companions: First-born children were more likely to have a companion. Only two other factors were associated with the presence of imaginary companions: increased self-initiated play and engagement in a greater number of different family-play activities.

Thus, despite the systematic nature of the Manosevitz et al. (1973) study, very little specific information was obtained regarding the factors associated with imaginary companions. Two explanations may account for these results. First, the age range of the sample was restricted—only 3- to 5-year-old children were included. Because previous researchers (e.g., Ames & Learned, 1946; Hurlock & Burstein, 1932) have reported the presence of imaginary companions in children up to 9 years of age, some of the factors associated with the presence of these companions may not have been apparent in younger children.

Second, questions regarding children's involvement in fantasy were not included in the original questionnaire. From a cognitive perspective, this oversight may have resulted in the exclusion of information. According to cognitive-affective theory, children use fantasy play as a method of assimilating new experiences into available schemata that reduce the fearfulness of an incongruous event and promote positive emotions, such as interest or excitement, that permit exploration (D. G. Singer & Singer, 1990). Within this theoretical framework, the imaginary companion may be viewed as a fantasy figure that assists children to assimilate and explore new experiences (D. G. Singer & Singer, 1990; Somers & Yawkey, 1984; Taylor, Cartwright, & Carlson, 1993).

Consideration of these two issues suggests that additional insight regarding the role of imaginary companions may be provided by extending the age range to include older children and by obtaining information regarding children's involvement in fantasy. In addition, consideration of the problems associated with imaginary companion research necessitates the use of a method that permits meaningful comparisons with previous findings. Thus, for the present study, we modified the questionnaire used by Manosevitz et al. (1973) and used it to investigate the prevalence and characteristics of children with imaginary companions.

Specifically, with the modified questionnaire, we sought to investigate (a) the prevalence of children with imaginary companions, (b) the family structures of children with and without imaginary companions, (c) the personality and behavioral characteristics of children with and without imaginary companions, (d) the patterns of play of children with and without imaginary companions, and (e) the incorporation of myth (as a measure of fantasy) in the daily lives of children with and without imaginary companions.

Two outcomes were expected in addition to those that would assist in evaluating information provided by the results of the Manosevitz et al. (1973) study. First, we expected that the inclusion of fantasy items would indicate an association between the presence of imaginary companions and children's predisposition to engage in fantasy. Second, we expected that extending the age range would provide information indicating that the effects of imaginary companions continue beyond the preschool years.

METHOD

Participants

The questionnaire used in this study was distributed through preschool and school centers to the parents of 900 children. The final sample on which the analysis was based totaled 478 children. There were 237 girls (M age = 5 years 9 months, range 2 years 2 months to 9 years 5 months) and 241 boys (M age = 5 years 11 months, range 2 years 6 months to 9 years 3 months). Within this sample, 81 children were reported to either have or have had an imaginary companion (M age = 5 years 6 months, range 2 years 9 months to 8 years 7 months); 397 children were reported as not having or never having had an imaginary companion (M age = 6 years 0 months, range 2 years 2 months to 9 years 5 months).

Because of concerns that questions about income might be considered intrusive, we used parents' education level, rather than financial status, as an indicator of socioeconomic background. In particular, mother's education level was used because, according to Entwisle and Astone (1994), it is rarely missing from surveys and has been found to be highly correlated with father's education level.

The education levels of the mothers in the present study indicated that the respondents were not fully representative of the general population for the area: 26% of the mothers reported an education level of some high school, 36% reported an education level of high school, and 38% reported an education level of university. In contrast, the percentage of respondents found at these education levels in the general population was 66%, 14%, and 8%, respectively (Australian Bureau of Statistics, 1991). Thus, despite our efforts to obtain a representative sample by distributing the questionnaire to children from a range of socioeconomic backgrounds, a large percentage of the respondents who completed and returned the questionnaire were educated beyond high school. Consequently, the sample in this study is weighted toward more highly educated families.

Questionnaire

The Imaginative Play Activities Questionnaire was developed for this study. This questionnaire consisted of four sections: (a) demographic data, (b) children's play activities and behavior, (c) mythical beings, and (d) imaginary companions. Sections 1, 2, and 4 were derived from the Imaginary Companion Questionnaire developed by Manosevitz et al. (1973) and were incorporated in slightly modified form into the current questionnaire. Section 3 was added to provide specific data regarding a child's exposure, incorporation in play, and beliefs concerning mythical beings (e.g., Santa Claus).

The modifications to Sections 1, 2, and 4 included changing and adding items that were more applicable to the present day (e.g., changing phonograph to CD/record player; including computer games); rewording items and phrases to suit Australian English (e.g., check to tick); deleting items that may be considered to have an intrusive quality and were not required (e.g., death of a child or spouse); and dividing questions that sought information on two issues concurrently (e.g., child's contact with music and literature).

Specific information was requested in each section. Section 1 requested information regarding family composition and parents' education. Section 2 requested information regarding the child's (a) friends (i.e., age, sex, and number), (b) style of play and interaction with others, (c) exposure to music and literature, (d) type and number of toys, and (e) existence of any behavioral problems. Section 3 requested information regarding the extent of the child's (a) exposure to mythical beings through stories and traditions, (b) belief in mythical beings and their reaction to the denial by others of their existence, and (c) imaginativeness and use of mythical characters in pretend play and story telling. Finally, Section 4 requested information concerning imaginary companions and covered the following topics: (a) age when the companion appeared and, if relevant, disappeared; (b) age, number, and type (e.g., nonhuman vs. human); (c) interaction between the child and the companion; and (d) parents' attitudes toward the companion.

After Section 2 was completed, the parents were provided with both a definition and examples of mythical beings. For this research, mythical beings were defined as fictional characters, such as Santa Claus and elves, around whom stories and cultural traditions have arisen. This definition, combined with the examples, allowed the parents to determine whether the fictional characters and traditions experienced by the child were mythical.

The final section dealt with imaginary companions. An imaginary companion was defined as a very vivid imaginary character that does not actually exist but is treated as real by the child, who plays with it and refers to it in conversation throughout the day. This definition allowed the parents to exclude the transient characters or objects that children use in pretend play and determine whether their child had an imaginary companion. Those parents whose child had an imaginary companion completed this section. Those whose child did not have an imaginary companion were instructed to proceed to the "optional" page at the end of the questionnaire.

Because the questionnaire could be returned anonymously, the optional page was for those parents who were interested in discussing their child's participation in future studies. We provided a choice in order to promote an acceptable return rate and allowed parents to return the questionnaire anonymously if they wished.

Procedure

After we had obtained approval from the institutional ethics committee, we delivered questionnaires to 11 centers (kindergartens, day-care centers, preschools, and primary schools) in the Hobart, Australia, metropolitan area. These centers covered the range of socioeconomic backgrounds (Australian Bureau of Statistics, 1991). Enrollments ranged from 31 to 209. Initial contact with these centers was conducted via the telephone and was followed by a personal visit to each in order to enlist participation.

The questionnaires were distributed by staff to the parents of all enrolled children. Each center was provided with a post box as a drop-off point for the completed questionnaires. In addition, each questionnaire was accompanied by an envelope and a cover letter that briefly explained the nature of the research and asked parents to place the completed questionnaires in the box provided at each center. Parents were assured that all information would be treated in the strictest confidence. After 10 days, a follow-up letter was sent to all parents urging them to complete and return the questionnaire if they had not already done so.

Results

The prevalence rate for parents' reports of imaginary companions was computed for the entire sample. Within the entire sample, 35 (7%) children were reported as having one or more imaginary companions, 46 (10%) were reported as having had one or more imaginary companions in the past, and 397 (83%) were reported as never having had an imaginary companion. Because the low numbers in each imaginary-companion group would have rendered separate analyses unreliable (Siegel & Castellan, 1988), we combined the past and present companion groups to form one imaginary companion group for the analyses.

Analyses

Analyses of categorical variables were conducted with chi-square tests. Because of the large difference in the numbers in each group, percentages are referred to in the text for clarity. However, all analyses were based on frequency data. All frequency data from the categorical variables were cast into 2×2 ($df = 1$)

contingency tables. Contingency tables that were larger than 2 × 2 were collapsed to deal with small expected frequencies. These tests were corrected for continuity, and the phi coefficient (ϕ) was used to measure the strength of association between variables. Because ϕ measures the strength of this association on a scale from 0 to 1, values close to 0 should be interpreted to indicate a weak relationship between variables, values close to 1 should be interpreted to indicate a strong relationship between variables, and values halfway between 0 and 1 should be interpreted to indicate a moderate relationship between variables (Diekhoff, 1992; Howell, 1987; Siegel & Castellan, 1988).

We conducted t tests for numerically scored variables such as the total number of behavior problems, level of imaginativeness, personality characteristics, and the ability to interact with adults and children. Equality of variance of the groups in the t test was assessed with the Levene test.

Results that are significant at an alpha level of .05 are reported. However, because of concerns that this alpha level may result in a Type I error, findings that were significant at .05 but not at more stringent alpha levels should be interpreted with caution.

Family Structure

The family structures of children with imaginary companions (IC) and children with no imaginary companions (NIC) were measured on four dimensions: number of siblings, birth order, number of any additional household members (e.g., aunts, uncles), and parents' relationship status.

In the IC group, 13% of the children were reported to come from homes in which parents were divorced, separated, or other (e.g., deceased or single parents), compared with 20% of the children in the NIC group. This difference was not significant.

Similarly, analyses of the number of siblings and the number of additional household members revealed no significant differences between ICs and NICs.

However, analysis of birth order revealed that a significantly larger percentage (29%) of ICs than NICs (14%) were reported to be first-born children, $\chi^2(1, N= 478) = 14.75, p < .001, \phi = .18$.

Education Level

The percentages of mothers of IC and NIC children who reported qualifications at each education level were not significantly different.

Styles of Play and Patterns of Interaction with Friends

The styles of play and patterns of friendship interactions of IC and NIC children were measured on four dimensions: the number of friends, the number of hours spent per day in play with friends, the style of play, and interaction during play with other children. The percentages of ICs and NICs who were reported to have one or more friends, spend up to 10 hr in play with these friends, frequently disagree with other children, and engage in self-initiated or quiet play were not significantly different.

However, analysis of how often and how well ICs and NICs played with other children revealed a significant difference between the two groups. In the NIC group, 91% of the children were reported to play often and well with other children, compared with 82% of the children in the IC group, $\chi^2(1, N = 478) = 5.35, p < .05, \phi = .11$.

Patterns of Interaction with the Family

The patterns of family interaction that were reported for IC and NIC children were measured on three dimensions: the number of hours spent per day with mother, the number of hours spent per day with father, and the number of activities that were engaged in jointly per day with family members.

The percentages of ICs and NICs who were reported to spend up to 6 hr with mother and with father were not significantly different. Similarly, the percentages of ICs and NICs who were reported to participate jointly in two or more activities with mother, with father, and with the family group were not significantly different.

However, a significantly larger percentage of NICs (71%) than ICs (59%) was reported to engage in two or more activities with siblings, $\chi^2(1, N = 478) = 4.02, p < .05, \phi = .10$.

Behavior Problems

A list of 22 behaviors was presented, and parents were asked to check any behavior problems that "are giving parents concern at present or have given concern in the past." Examples of the behaviors that were listed include restlessness, daydreaming, and lack of self-confidence. (See Appendix for a complete list of these behaviors.)

The total number of behavior problems that were reported for ICs and NICs was computed by summing every checked item for each IC and NIC group. The mean number of behavior problems was then calculated for each IC and NIC group. A t test revealed that there was no significant difference between these means (IC: $M = 1.31$, $SD = .89$; NIC: $M = 1.13$, $SD = .89$), $t(476) = -1.63$, p = u10, Levene test, $p = .99$.

Personality Characteristics

The personality characteristics of IC and NIC children were rated on four personality dimensions: imaginativeness, ability to talk and interact with adults, ability to talk and interact with children, and shyness. Each of these dimensions was rated on a 7-point scale ranging from very positive (I) to very negative (7).

T tests were performed to compare parents' ratings of IC and NIC children on each of the four personality dimensionsu These tests revealed that there were no significant differences in ratings of the abilities of ICs and NICs to talk and interact with adults, $t(476) = .46, p = .64$; to talk and interact with children, $t(476) = -.05, p = .96$; and of their degrees of shyness, $t(476) = -.94, p = .35$. However, the mean parent rating of level of imaginativeness for ICs was significantly lower than for NICs (IC: M = 1.48, SD = .59; NIC: M = 2.00, SD = .98); t(476) = 4.47, $p < .001$, Levene test, p = .57, indicating that the IC group had a higher degree of imaginativeness than the NIC group.

Involvement in Music and Stories

The involvement in music and stories of IC and NIC children was measured on two dimensions: general reaction to music and general reaction to literature. The percentages of ICs and NICs who were reported to participate actively or listen quietly to music and literature were not significantly different.

Involvement in Myth

The involvement in myth of IC and NIC children was measured on seven dimensions: frequently reads (or is read) stories involving mythical characters, is involved in mythical traditions, believes in mythical beings, angrily denies challenges to mythical belief, makes up stories of mythical beings, involves mythical beings in play, and explains events as magical.

The percentages of ICs and NICs who were reported to have mythical stories read frequently to them were not significantly different. Similarly, the percentages of ICs and NICs who were reported to be involved in mythical traditions, believe in mythical beings, and angrily deny challenges to mythical belief were not significantly different.

However, 68% of ICs, compared with 42% NICs, were reported to make up stories of mythical beings that did not include the imaginary companion, $\chi^2(1, N = 478) = 17.74$, $p < .001$, $\phi = .20$; 57% of ICs, compared with 32% of NICs, were reported to involve mythical beings other than the imaginary companion in play, $\chi^2(1, N = 478) = 16.47$, $p < .001$, $\phi = .19$; and 46% of ICs, compared with 32% of NICs, were reported to explain events as magical, $\chi^2(1, N = 478) = 5.00$, $p < .05$, $\phi = .11$.

Imaginary Companions

The next phase of the analysis dealt with the questionnaire data that were obtained from the parents of children with imaginary companions (n = 81). The first analysis was conducted to determine the existence of any gender differences with regard to the number of companions experienced by boys and girls.

The total numbers of imaginary companions—male, female, and of nonspecific gender—that were reported for girls and boys did not differ significantly. However, a significantly larger number of male companions were reported for boys than for girls (IC as male: boys, M = .46, SD = .51; girls, M = .23, SD = .42), t(79) = 2.25, $p < .05$, Levene test, p = .0005; and a significantly larger number of female companions were reported for girls than for boys (IC as female: girls, M = .57, SD = .50; boys, M = .32, SD = .48), t(79) = −2.23, $p < .05$, Levene test, p = .06. These results should be treated with caution because the Levene tests indicate that the group variances were not equal.

Additional descriptive data that were obtained from parents whose children had an imaginary companion are summarized in Table 1. Of particular interest were the findings that the imaginary companion was a being whose age was unknown (37%), the same as the child's (43%), or older than the child's (20%). The majority of children played happily (78%) with their companions, played in the home (88%) with them, and ignored the companion when other children were present (83%).

The attitudes of parents toward the imaginary companion were mostly positive. Only 1 parent referred to the companion as harmful. The other parents either regarded the companion as good for the child (66%) or as having no effect (33%). A similar pattern of results was found for parental treatment of the companion: 73% of the parents encouraged having the companion, 24% ignored the companion, and only 3% discouraged having the companion.

DISCUSSION

We used a modified version of a previously developed method to promote meaningful comparisons between the present study and previous research regarding the prevalence and characteristics of children with imaginary companions. We also explored the possibility of an association between the presence of imaginary companions and children's involvement in fantasy, as well as the possibility that the effects of imaginary companions continue beyond the preschool years.

The findings of the present study indicate that IC and NIC children do not differ significantly on the majority of measures. However, the study did reveal significant differences between IC and NIC children regarding their birth order, level of imaginativeness, and predisposition to engage in fantasy. These findings are consistent with those of previous research (e.g., Ames & Learned, 1946; Manosevitz et al., 1973; Taylor et al., 1993). We found that IC children were more often reported to be very imaginative and to be firstborns compared with NIC children. The significant difference in the number of reported firstborns in the IC and NIC groups substantiates the view that one function of the imaginary companion may be to ameliorate the loneliness of a child who does not have any siblings close in age (Manosevitz et al., 1973). In addition, children with ICs were more often reported to make up stories about mythical beings that did not include the imaginary companion, involve mythical beings other than the imaginary companion in play, and explain events as magical. As a measure of fantasy, these results corroborate previous research findings that children with ICs have a strong tendency to engage in fantasy play spontaneously (Taylor & Carlson, 1997; Taylor et al., 1993).

Table 1. Summary of Questionnaire Data From Parents of Children with Imaginary Companions (n = 81)

Question	% Giving Response
Type of companion	
Person	77
Animal and other	23
Same-sex companion	
Boys	46
Girls	57
Number of companions	
1	59
2	21
Age of companion	
Unknown	37
Same age as the child	43
Older than the child	20
Parental attitude	
Good for the child	66
No effect on the child	33
Harmful for the child	1
Frequency of appearance of imaginary companions	
Steady companion, appears almost every day	46
Appears frequently but not everyday	42
Appeared only once or twice	7
Mood of child when talking or playing with imaginary companion	
Happy and in high spirits	78
Quiet and reserved	4
Lonely	3
Angry	3
No specific mood	12
Origin of names of imaginary companion	
Friend	21
Television	12
Interaction with companion	
Preferred not to interact with imaginary companion when other children were available	83
Nature of relationship between imaginary companion and child	
Usually play peacefully together	85

(*Continued*)

Table 1. (*Continued*)

QUESTION	% GIVING RESPONSE
Sometimes have arguments and disagreements	17
At times child consults or asks permission of imaginary companion before doing something	25
At times the imaginary companion asks permission of the child to do something	21
Child uses imaginary companion to escape blame	25
Places and activities that imaginary companion usually accompanies the child	
Outside	62
In home	88
Driving in car	52
While eating	35
While shopping	27
To and at preschool/school	14
To bed	48
While watching television	12
Talks on telephone to imaginary companion	32
Physical space imaginary companion occupies	
Needs its own chair at the table	25
Needs place in child's bed	32
Needs room in the car	36
Needs space of its own, various places other than those specified above	10
Does not need any space	48
Parental behavior that prompted appearance of the imaginary companion	
Punishment or scolding	9
Requiring child to play indoors or in his/her room	10
Parent unable to attend to child	22
Questioning child or expressing interest in an imaginary companion	36
Other	20
Parental treatment of imaginary companion	
Encourage the companion	73
Discourage the companion	3
Ignore the companion	24
Disappearance of imaginary companion	
Child gradually stopped playing and talking to imaginary companion	37
When child started preschool	12
Imaginary companion left suddenly without explanation	24
Imaginary companion disappeared after a fight	0
Imaginary companion moved away or died	5

This predisposition to fantasy, combined with the finding in this study that the majority of children were reported to be happy when playing with the companion, suggests that another function of the imaginary companion may be to assist children to assimilate new information into available schemata by creating a positively reinforcing atmosphere for exploration (D. G. Singer & Singer, 1990).

This study also revealed differences between IC and NIC children in their interactions with family members and other children. These findings are not consistent with those of some previous reports (e.g., Manosevitz et al., 1973; Mauro, 1990; J. L. Singer, 1973; D. G. Singer & Singer, 1990). We found that, compared with IC children, NIC children were reported to engage in more activities with siblings and to play often and well with other children. These findings suggest that IC children are less sociable than NIC children. However, because children with imaginary companions were more often reported to be firstborns, age differences may have prevented a significant proportion of these children from engaging in many activities with their younger siblings. In addition, in contrast to second-born or subsequent children, who may play with older siblings in the family context, first-born children do not have immediate access to brothers or sisters. Consequently, these children may have had less experience playing with others.

The prevalence rate of children with imaginary companions was also found to be much lower in this study than in studies reported by other researchers (see Manosevitz et al., 1973; Mauro, 1990; D. G. Singer & Singer, 1990). There are two explanations that may account for this low prevalence rate. First, in order to encourage as many parents as possible to return the questionnaire and provide a more accurate estimate of the incidence of imaginary companions, we deliberately designed the questionnaire to obtain information on all children's play activities and did not focus solely on imaginary companions. As a consequence of its broad emphasis, the questionnaire targeted all parents and increased the likelihood of obtaining responses from parents whose children did not have imaginary companions. In contrast, the questionnaire that was used by Manosevitz et al. (1973) focused specifically on the topic of imaginary companions, thus targeting the parents of children who had these companions and increasing the likelihood that these parents would respond.

Second, we used parent reports in the present study. Previous researchers (e.g., Brooks & Knowles, 1982; Mauro, 1990; D. G. Singer & Singer, 1990) have suggested that parents are a poor source of information regarding imaginary companions. According to these views, parents either report inaccurate details regarding their child's companion or demonstrate a bias against reporting its presence.

However, subsequent interview research conducted by one of the present authors did not substantiate these views. Information gathered from 37 NIC children in the present study, randomly selected from those families who agreed to further participation, indicated that parents had provided accurate information regarding the absence of imaginary companions for their children.

In all 37 cases, the children's responses to the interview questions confirmed the parent report data. Thus, we argue that the reported prevalence rate of imaginary companions in the present study is an accurate reflection of the prevalence of imaginary companions among children generally, rather than an outcome of inaccuracies and biases.

In summary, the results of this study and of previous imaginary companion research (e.g., Ames & Learned, 1946; Manosevitz et al., 1973) suggest that birth order combined with personality characteristics such as imaginativeness and a predisposition to fantasy are significant factors in the occurrence of imaginary companions. In addition, the data that were obtained in this study support the interpretation that imaginary companions may function to alleviate loneliness and promote emotional and cognitive growth by creating a positive atmosphere for exploration (D. G. Singer & Singer, 1990). Moreover, the inclusion of older children in the sample suggests that imaginary companions and their effects extend beyond the preschool years.

APPENDIX

The 22 Behaviors in the Imaginative Play Activities Questionnaire

Restlessness
Nailbiting
Overactivity
Nose picking
Hair pulling or twisting
Masturbation
Jealousy
Fearfulness
Aggressiveness
Competitiveness
Irritability
Shyness
Excitability
Thumb-sucking
Flightiness
Awkwardness
Submissiveness
Daydreaming
Overdependence on adults

Undue demand for attention

Lack of self-confidence

Sensitiveness

The authors thank all of the centers and parents of children who cooperated and participated in this study.

CRITICAL THINKING QUESTIONS

1. What were the two hypotheses proposed by the researchers? What evidence was presented that would either support or refute these hypotheses?
2. Looking at the tables regarding imaginary friends, what conclusions would you come to regarding prevalence and typical developmental patterns of imaginary friends?
3. Based on this research do you think parents should be concerned if their child has an imaginary friend? Would there be any situations in which they should be concerned?

REFERENCES

Ames, L. B., & Learned, J. (1946). Imaginary companions and related phenomena. *The Journal of Genetic Psychology,* 69, 147–167.

Australian Bureau of Statistics. (1991). Census 1991 (No. 2791.6). Canberra, Australian Capital Territory: Author.

Brooks, M., & Knowles, D. (1982). Parents' views of children's imaginary companions. *Child Welfare,* LXI, 25–33.

Diekhoff, G. (1992). *Statistics for the social and behavioral sciences: Univariate, bivariate, multivariate.* Dubuque, IA: Wm. C. Brown.

Entwisle, D. R., & Astone, N.M. (1994). Some practical guidelines for measuring youth's race/ethnicity and socioeconomic status. *Child Development,* 65, 1521–1540.

Fraiberg, S. (1968). *The magic years.* New York: Scribner's.

Howell, D.C. (1987). *Statistical methods for psychology* (2nd ed.). Boston: PWS-Kent.

Hurlock, E. B., & Burstein, M. (1932). The imaginary playmate: A questionnaire study. *The Journal of Genetic Psychology,* 41, 380–392.

Jalongo, M. (1984). Imaginary companions in children's lives and literature. *Childhood Education,* 60, 166–171.

Jersild, A. T. (1968). *Child psychology* (6th ed.). Englewood Cliffs, NJ: Prentice-Hall.

Jersild, A. T., Markey, F. V., & Jersild, C. L. (1933). Children's fears, dreams, wishes, daydreams, likes, dislikes, pleasant and unpleasant memories. *Child Development Monographs.* New York: Bureau of Publications, Teacher's College, Columbia University.

Manosevitz, M., Prentice, N.M., & Wilson, E (1973). Individual and family correlates of imaginary companions in preschool children. *Developmental Psychology*, 8, 72–79.

Mauro, J. (1990). The friend that only I can see: A longitudinal investigation of children's imaginary companions. Unpublished doctoral dissertation, University of Oregon, Eugene.

Siegel, S., & Castellan, N.J. (1988). *Nonparametric statistics for the behavioral sciences* (2nd ed.). New York: McGraw-Hill.

Singer, D. G., & Singer, J. L. (1990). *The house of make-believe: Children's play and the developing imagination.* Cambridge, MA: Harvard University Press.

Singer, J. L. (1961). Imagination and waiting ability in young children. *Journal of Personality*, 29, 396–413.

Singer, J. L. (1973). *The child's world of make-believe: Experimental studies of imaginative play.* San Diego: Academic Press.

Singer, J. L., & Singer, D. G. (1981). *Television, imagination and aggression: A study of preschoolers.* Hillsdale, NJ: Erlbaum.

Somers, J. U., & Yawkey, T. D. (1984). Imaginary play companions: Contributions of creative and intellectual abilities of young children. *Journal of Creative Behaviour,* 18, 77–89.

Taylor, M., & Carlson, S. M. (1997). The relation between individual differences in fantasy and theory of mind. *Child Development,* 68, 436–455.

Taylor, M., Cartwright, B. S., & Carlson, S. M. (1993). A developmental investigation of children's imaginary companions. *Developmental Psychology,* 29, 276–285.

Vostrovsky, C. (1895). A study of imaginary companions. *Education,* 15, 393–398.

10

Early Childhood: Social and Emotional Development

Childreach: Violence Prevention in Preschool Settings

Trena Goodwin, Katheryn Pacey, and Mary Grace

TOPIC. Early intervention to decrease violent and aggressive behavior in preschool-age children.
PURPOSE. To describe a model of an on-site early identification and intervention program for children under 6 in child care and preschool settings.
SOURCES. Literature review, authors' experiences in preschool prevention services, and pre/post intervention data using standardized toots.
CONCLUSIONS. An on-site secondary prevention program is an effective strategy to decrease violent and aggressive behavior in very young children. This model can be replicated in most communities through collaborations among childhood mental health professionals and early childhood educators.

Journal of Child and Adolescent Psychiatric Nursing, April–June 2003, v16, i2, p52(9).

© 2003 Blackwell Publishing. inc.

More young children are spending time in early childhood education programs or child care settings. The percentage of preschool children under 5 who are cared for in child care centers jumped from 1 in 20 in 1965 to 3 in 10 by the 1990s (Scarr, 1998). Early childhood programs fill a void and often are at the forefront in recognizing the child at risk for later social or emotional difficulties that stem from poor peer relationships or alienation—difficulties that can prove fertile ground for later pathologies. Research indicates that more than 10% of elementary school-age children have no friendship nominations from peers (Hymel, Wagner, & Butler, 1990). For the preschool child, limited in insight and desperate for a sense of belonging, social alienation can quickly escalate into negative behaviors and increase feelings of isolation. Research has begun to identify some of the causal risk factors for early school failure. These include (a) cognitive deficits, (b) early behavior problems, (c) parental psychological problems, (d) problematic parenting practices, and (e) difficulties with peers and teachers (Figure 1). (All figures referenced can be found within the online version of this article, at http://www.infotrac-college.com.)

Children who are socially and emotionally immature at kindergarten entry are at greater risk for school failure during the early elementary school years (Child Mental Health Foundation and Agencies Network [FAN], 2000). Kindergarten teachers indicate that close to half the children who enter kindergarten display either academic, behavioral, or social risk factors that potentially jeopardize school progress during the early elementary school years (Huffman, Mehlinger, & Kerivan, 2000). Professionals in mental health, education, social service agencies, and the juvenile court systems now recognize that early identification and intervention is a necessary part in the prevention of mental health problems (U.S. Department of Health and Human Services, 1999). Early intervention may be critical in redirecting a child's negative coping strategies to more positive ones before the child encounters the rigors of elementary school.

Childreach—an early identification, short-term intervention program for children under the age of 6—is designed to address aggression as well as other behavioral issues. The most common referring behavior to the Childreach program is hostility or violence in the preschool classroom. Early identification of aggressive behavior is critical. Children who do not receive intervention for their aggressive behavior in preschool are likely to continue their aggressive behavior in elementary school. For children, acts of violence often escalate over rime, peak in mid-adolescence, and begin to decline by adulthood. But research demonstrates that children who are violent are more likely to remain so as adults (Kazdin, 1997).

In Ohio, research findings presented by Hamilton County Family and Children First Council (2000) indicated that as many as 1 in 10 children met the criteria for poor emotional or behavioral health and often fell into a category of children who are at risk for later difficulties as they proceed through elementary school. Atypical behaviors at preschool age stem from a variety of sources that may include developmental delay, problems of adjustment, and emerging mental health needs.

Dealing with the preschool child also poses a dilemma of knowing when a behavior is a slight delay in development or when it is atypical and in need of professional intervention. For young children, mental health needs often present as aggression. Young children often have not developed the ability to express themselves verbally. Aggression may reflect frustration that stems from a lack of developmental mastery in language or a deficit in self-regulation. Altemately, aggression may be the result of a mismatch in a child's developmental level and environmental demands or an inability to adjust to the expected behavior in a specific setting. Many young children have not yet learned to manage their daily stressors and channel them into appropriate behavior. A child's ability to successfully navigate the earlier years of developmental milestones also may be compromised by prenatal, genetic, or physiological factors. Aggression also may reflect what a child sees, either through the media or within daily life. At present, researchers continue to struggle to identify the behaviors associated with exposure to violence (Commission for the Prevention of Youth Violence, 2000). Thus, the factors that contribute to a preschooler's poor adjustment and aggressive presentation are complex and may include a variety of sources in isolation or combination, including developmental delays, self-regulation issues, life events, psychiatric disorders, social skill deficits, language delays, and temperament, as well as factors within the child's environment.

PROGRAM DEVELOPMENT

The Childreach program was created in 1995 following a request to Hamilton County Community Mental Health Board from the early childhood education community in Cincinnati at a time when some children in the early childhood centers were exhibiting severe, aggressive behaviors. Early childhood directors and teachers were finding it increasingly difficult to manage these children's behaviors and were excluding them from their child care programs in order to keep a safe environment. Frequently, the child care staff members were new to the early childhood field and inexperienced, and did not recognize these behaviors as signs of emotional distress in young children. Although some of the more experienced teachers could identify children with beginning signs of emotionally based behavior disorders, they did not know how to intervene to improve the behaviors. In addition, many of these teachers needed a mental health professional to frame a child's misbehavior and need for intervention in a palatable way the parents would hear, absorb, and be willing to accept.

Childreach was designed to be a primary and secondary prevention program. The program emphasis was on identifying early signs and symptoms of the children's behaviors before they reached the point that required the child seek mental health treatment or be excluded from child care. This goal required a program structured to address needs on several levels. A focal consideration was parents' needs. Most parents are not ready to see their preschool-age child as having behavior problems, let alone a formal mental health diagnosis, and are reluctant to seek treatment for the child. We realized in this community that even if the parent agrees to seek treatment for the child, most of the third-party payers do not have treatment providers on their panels who have expertise with children under the age of 5. We also realized many of the referred behaviors could be linked to the fact that early childhood teachers are not trained to manage severe behavior problems. Thus, one aim of Childreach was to create preschool and child care center-based services that could help teachers understand and improve the ways they manage the children's behaviors. This type of service requires a great deal of time and is often not billable to a third-party payer, but is crucial to helping change the child's behavior.

Childreach was created to address these needs. Childreach is part of the Prevention and Education Center of Central Clinic, a nonprofit, outpatient, community mental health center affiliated with the University of Cincinnati, Department of Psychiatry. Childreach is an expansion of two of Central Clinic's prevention services: the school outreach prevention services for students in grades K–12 that have been provided for more than 20 years, and the early outreach identification services, a longtime consultation service to area child care centers and preschools. The funding for Childreach comes mainly from the Hamilton County Community Mental Health Board and United Way, with support from some other time-limited grants. Services are offered to any child 5 years old and under who is enrolled atone of a hundred child care centers and preschools or in a home-child care provider's care. Childreach established a collaborative partnership among three agencies providing clinical, consultation, and training services: Central Clinic and Talbert House, both mental health agencies, and 4-C, an early childhood education, training, and referral agency.

PROGRAM DESIGN

Our current service delivery model (Figure 2) evolved over several years. The process begins with a referral from the child care center director or parent and moves through a series of steps designed to shape services around the child's needs. Having provided consultation to the early childhood community for many years, we understood that a comprehensive approach was needed to make a significant impact on the child's behavior, one that would enable him or her to remain in the child care setting.

An effective design for providing on-site early childhood intervention services demands consideration of the gestalt of the child's world: the internal world of the child, his or her interaction with their family, family life events and their effects on him or her, the quality of his or her experience with other children, and relationships with adults in the child care environment. All these pieces must be working together to give children the support they need to thrive. Services to address these different points of need include consultation to the staff and parents, intervention to an individual child and family (at home or at the child care agency), staff training, parent training, and referral liaison services. An effective intervention strategy also needs to address the child's behavior and its precipitants, the behavior-management strategies implemented by the parents and child care staff, the level of knowledge and experience of the child care staff, the cognitive/developmental level of the child, the physical environment of the child care setting/classroom, and whether the family is able to meet the child's emotional needs.

Intervention also involves balancing the work with the child's family and the school environment. While working with the child and family to understand the child's behavior and make some changes in the family, we also are working with child care staff to develop appropriate expectations of the child and use more effective behavior-management strategies. Child care staff needs continuous support while the Childreach staff works with the child and parents to effect change in the child's behavior. This dual focus is the key to supporting the classroom unit, so the child remains in the classroom while changes are occurring.

REFERRAL AND INTERVENTION PROCESS

A child may be referred for Childreach services in a variety of ways. The most common referral route is when a child care center director identifies that he or she needs help with a child's behavior and calls the Childreach staff. Sometimes the referral comes from center staff following a Childreach training they have attended about an early childhood education topic, such as managing severe temper tantrums or helping young children use their words instead of hitting. Sometimes the referral comes directly from the parent who is concerned about his or her child's behavior.

After the child care center director has obtained written parent permission, the initial consultation visit to the center is scheduled. During this first visit to the center, the Childreach worker gathers the staff's concerns about the child's behavior, asks the staff to complete the initial Child and Adolescent Adjustment Profile (CAAP, described in detail below), and does an initial observation of the child in the classroom. In addition to monitoring the behaviors for which the child is referred, the goal of the observation is to assess the classroom environment, including interactions among the children and teachers. The worker notes multiple aspects of the environment, such as file types of materials available to the child for stimulation, the physical set-up of the classroom, and the structure and daily schedule. Also observed are how choices are given and made during activities and meal-time, and if the class environment feels calm and soothing, or loud and chaotic. Finally the worker notes the teacher's approach to conflict resolution, the tone of voice and use of words by the staff, and the attitude of the staff toward the child's behavior.

This first consultation may take 3 to 4 hours, giving the consultant adequate time to see the child in a variety of activities at different times of day. Two more observations usually are completed before scheduling the parent-staff conference. We have found that parents have more confidence in the consultant's findings and recommendations if they know an extensive observation of their child and the center was conducted.

The parent conference includes the parents, center director, classroom teacher, and the consultant. The consultant facilitates a nonblaming discussion among all participants, giving them the opportunity to voice their concerns and to gain understanding of the needs of the child. Agreement is reached regarding some interventions to try at home and in the classroom. Every effort is made to support parents and staff around the work with this child. Often, additional family needs are identified at this conference, such as therapy for the parents, staff training, or parent education.

Visits are then scheduled for the consultant to return to the child care center and to assess if the interventions have made a difference in the child's behavior or if there is a need for additional visits. At this point, if no gains are evident, interventions may be revised or a referral made for additional services. On occasion, if the need is apparent, the decision to refer a child for other services may be made prior to attempting interventions. The whole process takes approximately 3 months. Consultation visits are spaced far enough apart to give the child, family, and center staff adequate time to implement suggestions and see change. At the end of 3 months the center director again completes the CAAP and a service satisfaction survey. Even though the consultation has been completed on a particular child, ongoing support is provided to the staff during visits to the child care center. At these times, the Childreach workers reinforce the changes the child has accomplished.

GROUP LEVEL FINDINGS

Since the inception of Childreach in 1995, more than 500 young children (75% boys, 38% African American) have been served in the program. The modal age of clients was 4 years (41%), an additiona1 32% were 3 years old or younger, and 27% were 5 years old. Improvement in behavior following Childreach intervention was measured using the CAAP (Ellsworth, 1981). The teacher-rated CAAP is a 20-item measure of adjustment that yields rive factors of adjustment: peer relations, dependency, hostility, productivity, and withdrawal. A pre/post method of assessment was used at the beginning and end of the intervention. This measure had adequate reliability and validity as described in the administration manual. Normative data on populations of children throughout the United States was available for comparison purposes.

As demonstrated in Figure 3, teacher-rated evaluations showed a significant improvement in all areas of behavior with the exception of dependence, a scale on which children initially showed only minimal impairment. Of particular interest clinically is the reduction in hostility scores, since these types of behaviors put the child at high risk for removal from the school. It is noteworthy that the reduction in hostility comes from a variety of interventions, depending on the nature of contributing factors. Most of the time, there was a parallel increase in the child's ability to play successfully with others and to become more productive in the preschool setting. It seems once hostility is reduced, frustration declines and the child is often able to get back to the real challenges of successful preschool development. The data demonstrate that, as a secondary prevention program that directs its energies toward a targeted group of children who have been identified as at risk, Childreach made a difference.

Another key outcome monitored in the Childreach program is expulsion (disenrollment) rates based on inappropriate classroom behavior. Among children served through the Childreach program, disenrollment rates have remained at less than 5% for the duration of the program. Directors report that even modest change in behaviors such as those measured by the CAAP, particularly in aggressive behaviors, often made the difference in retaining a child in the classroom. Preschool teachers and child care staff also reported extremely high levels of satisfaction with the Childreach program.

CASE STUDIES

An analysis of two case studies illustrates the complexity of young children's behavioral issues, as well as how difficult it can be to interpret the meaning behind their behavior.

Case study 1

In the words of her peers, 3-year-old Kelsey was "leaky." In the words of her teachers, Kelsey kept them from teaching. In the words of Kelsey, "Everybody else gots friends; all I gots is mad faces and sad drops!" In reality, they were all right. Plagued as she was with allergies, Kelsey's nose ran all the time and the medication she took made it hard for her to regulate her overabundance of energy. Because her nose was often stuffy, she breathed through her mouth, which made her drool. She was anxious and often in trouble from her poor self-regulation and, consequently, chewed on her shirtsleeve or the neck of her shirt. Kelsey had some residual toilet training delays stemming from her frequent illnesses as a toddler, and was often either damp or just plain wet in the seat of her pants. Socially, no one wanted to hold her hand, sit by her at lunch, or be her friend.

Frustrated by her lack of belongingness, Kelsey began to seek attention through negative behaviors like pushing, shoving, kicking, jumping on her naptime cot, sneaking, and crying most of the day. Kelsey, with her negative behaviors, still didn't have anyone to play with, but she was no longer ignored. Kelsey was at risk of being excluded from the early childhood program she attended, and the director had placed an extra aide in the class just to manage her behaviors. Over the next 3 months, the consultant worked with the teachers and parents to modify Kelsey's day in such a way that she had positive interactions with staff and shorter days. In addition, efforts were made to help Kelsey improve her hygiene and social skills so she could appropriately seek attention. With these changes, the children were more willing to play with her.

Case study 2

Richard was referred for defiance, opposition, and aggression. As he was observed one afternoon, he wandered aimlessly around a big gym. Thirty children were returning and playing. Balls were bouncing in all directions. The three teachers assigned to watch the children in the gymnasium were sitting on the sidelines, talking to one another about their day. Richard sat alone under the slide. No one came close to him. In a quick flash of energy, Richard ran around the slide, dashed up the ladder, and jumped from the top of the 6-foot slide to the floor at the end of the slide. No teacher intervened, so Richard, glancing toward the teachers, jumped to the end of the slide a second time. On his third jump, a child who had narrowly missed being hurt told the teacher, and Richard was chastised from across the gym. Once the children returned to their classroom, after at least 15 more minutes of play, Richard was placed in time-out at the back of the classroom while a movie blared at the front of the classroom in an effort to entertain the children while they were waiting for their parents. His teacher approached him and asked him if he had jumped off the slide. Richard looked down at the chair that he was sitting in and replied, "No, I sit in the chair." The exact conversation was repeated 15 times until time 16, when Richard kicked the teacher in frustration. The teacher reported to Richard's parents that he had jumped off the slide, lied about it, and kicked her when she tried to talk to him. Discussion about the slide took place too late, it was too long, it was not context based, and it was too abstract. Richard correctly answered the question he thought the teacher was asking 15 times before he kicked her.

An evaluation of Richard's language skills indicated his language was delayed by about 18 months and thus much of his aggression stemmed from the frustration he felt from not being able to follow, or appropriately respond to, his environment. In order to change his behavior, it was necessary to help Richard's teachers and parents understand better ways to communicate with him. The Childreach staff understood that a young child's behavior is hardly ever as simple as it appears, and it takes time and careful attention to understand the underlying dynamics.

DISCUSSION

The knowledge that children's experiences from birth to 5 years greatly determine their later behavior has made an early intervention program such as Childreach appealing to program and community planners. For those interested in implementing a similar program, we present lessons learned in program implementation, continuity of care, and agency collaboration. A key lesson of program implementation was the need to plan and structure funding so the needs of the population could be addressed adequately. For instance, we found five to six consultation sessions were frequently not enough to make the needed changes, especially for severely dysfunctional families and uneducated center staff. While outcomes indicate a reduction in hostility from the beginning to the completion of work with particular children, the overall level of hostility remained high. This suggested the need for additional sessions beyond the five to six already offered.

The program also demanded funding that allowed for flexibility in the services provided. Funding from public entities, such as the county mental health board or United Way, may not have the time limitations of a grant and provide a flexible base of funds to do both primary and secondary prevention activities needed with this young population. Building in a clear and measurable outcome process is critical to obtaining ongoing funding; it also makes a project for this age group more marketable.

Lessons learned also included continuity of care issues and the availability of ongoing service resources. An outreach program requires clinical back-up that, when needed, provides staff with support as well as additional clinical opinion. In line with this recommendation, because the therapeutic interventions for preschool children differ from those for the older child, an early intervention program needs clinicians adequately prepared in the area of early childhood mental health. Continuity of care issues became complicated because there were very few mental health providers in the community for us to refer a child who required ongoing treatment. This was especially true for families on private insurance panels.

Agency collaboration issues are complex. It is important to build collaborative relationships with the entire early childhood community, as it takes both the child care teachers and the mental health professionals to support these young families. In addition, early childhood teachers and child care staff need to be trained in how to address the social-emotional needs of young children. Each clinical Childreach worker was assigned to cover a particular child care center, thus facilitating relationships with center staff and parents. We found this collaboration established a positive tone of mutual learning. For example, Childreach workers presented content on how to help children with nonaggressive expression of feelings by modeling how to do social skills groups with the teachers present in the classroom. Childreach workers found teachers frequently had creative suggestions about how to design and implement a needed intervention for a particular child. In addition, the Childreach consultation process often stimulated the teacher to think of the problem behavior and solution in a fresh way.

After 6 years, we are encouraged with the progress of the program in meeting the early intervention needs of the preschool child. Longer follow-up of these children as they enter kindergarten and primary school will help us understand the long-term benefits of our program.

CRITICAL THINKING QUESTIONS

1. In what ways does Childreach provide preventative services to preschoolers that are both primary and secondary? Give examples of each.
2. Based on the data given in this article would you think that Childreach could be deemed an effective program for violence prevention in preschools? What other factors might need to be considered?
3. If you were conducting follow-up studies with the children included in this preschool program, what type of information would you want to know about these children as they entered elementary, junior high, and high school? How would you design these studies?

REFERENCES

The Child Mental Health Foundations and Agencies Network. (2000). *Off to a good start: Research on the risk factors for early school problems and selected federal policies affecting children's social and emotional development and their readiness for school.* Chapel Hill, NC: University of North Carolina, FPG Child Development Center.

Commission for the Prevention of Youth Violence. (2000). *Violence prevention medicine, nursing, and public health: Connecting the dots to prevent violence.* Chicago: American Medical Association.

Ellsworth, R.B. (1981). *The measurement of child and adolescent adjustment.* Palo Alto, CA: Consulting Psychologists Press.

Hamilton County Family and Children First Council. (2000). *Annual report.* Cincinnati, OH: Author.

Huffman, L., Mehlinger, S., & Kerivan, A. (2000). Risk factors for academic and behavioral problems at the beginning of school. In Child Mental Health Foundation & Agencies Network (Eds.), *Off to a good start: Research on the risk factors for each school problem and selected federal policies affecting children's social and emotional development and the readiness for school.* Chapel Hill, NC: University of North Carolina, FPG Child Development Center.

Hymel, S., Wagner, E., & Butler, L. (1990). Reputational bias: View from the peer group. In S.R. Asher & J.D. Cole (Eds.), *Peer rejection in childhood* (pp. 234–235). Cambridge, UK: Cambridge University Press.

Kazdin, A. (1997). Conduct disorder across the lifespan. In S. Luthar, J. Burack, D. Cicchetti, & J. Weisz, (Eds.), *Developmental psychopathology: Perspectives on adjustment, risk, and disorder* (pp. 248–272). Cambridge, UK: Cambridge University Press.

Scarr, S. (1998). American childcare today. *American Psychologist,* 53, 95–108.

U.S. Department of Health and Human Services. (1999). *Mental health: A report of the Surgeon General—Executive summary.* Rockville, MD: Author.

Trena Goodwin, APRN, MSN, LPCC, CNS, is Adjunct Associate Professor, University of Cincinnati, and Director of Prevention Services, Central Clinic, Cincinnati, OH. Katheryn Pacey, PhD, is Developmental Psychologist and Visiting Assistant Professor, University of Cincinnati Raymond Walters College, and in Private Practice, Cincinnati. Mary Grace, MEd, MS, is Sr. Research Associate, University of Cincinnati, and Director of Outcomes, Central Clinic, Cincinnati.

11

Middle Childhood: Physical Development

Health Consequences of Obesity in Youth: Childhood Predictors of Adult Disease

William H. Dietz

Obesity during childhood and adolescence can cause psychological and social problems, and may predispose young people to obesity and its health consequences as adults. Obese children tend to grow more quickly, and may be mistaken for older children and expected to behave accordingly. Children develop negative attitudes about overweight as young as 6 years old, and may exclude fat children from play. Obese youth can be at risk for diabetes, fatty liver, high blood pressure, and sleep apnea. Development of a negative body image in youth may lead to eating disorders, especially in girls.

Obesity now affects one in five children in the United States. Discrimination against overweight children begins early in childhood and becomes progressively institutionalized. Because obese children tend to be taller than their nonoverweight peers, they are apt to be viewed as more mature. The inappropriate expectations that result may have an adverse effect on their socialization. Many of the cardiovascular consequences that characterize

Health consequences of obesity in youth: childhood predictors of adult disease. (The Causes and Health Consequences of Obesity in Children and Adolescents). William H. Dietz From- *Pediatrics*, March 1998 v101, n3, p518(8). © 1998 American Academy of Pediatrics. Reproduced with Permission.

adult-onset obesity are preceded by abnormalities that begin in childhood. Hyperlipidemia, hypertension, and abnormal glucose tolerance occur with increased frequency in obese children and adolescents. The relationship of cardiovascular risk factors to visceral fat independent of total body fat remains unclear. Sleep apnea, pseudotumor cerebri, and Blount's disease represent major sources of morbidity for which rapid and sustained weight reduction is essential. Although several periods of increased risk appear in childhood, it is not clear whether obesity with onset early in childhood carries a greater risk of adult morbidity and mortality. Obesity is now the most prevalent nutritional disease of children and adolescents in the United States. Although obesity-associated morbidities occur more frequently in adults, significant consequences of obesity as well as the antecedents of adult disease occur in obese children and adolescents. In this review, I consider the adverse effects of obesity in children and adolescents and attempt to outline areas for future research. I refer to obesity as a body mass index greater than the 95th percentile for children of the same age and gender. (Pediatrics 1998;101:518–525; obesity, children, adolescents, consequences, comorbidity.)

The most widespread consequences of childhood obesity are psychosocial. Obese children become targets of early and systematic discrimination. As they mature, the effects of discrimination become more culture-bound and insidious. An important sequel of the widespread discrimination and cultural preoccupation with thinness is concern about weight expressed at young ages. The concern becomes part of the culture and is most pronounced among female dancers and gymnasts.

Several studies have shown clearly that children at a young age are sensitized to obesity and have begun to incorporate cultural preferences for thinness. Preference tests have demonstrated that 10- to 11-year-old boys and girls prefer as friends other children with a wide variety of handicaps to children who are overweight.[1] Overweight children are ranked lowest as those with whom they would like to be friends. Furthermore, children ranging in age from 6 to 10 years already associate obesity with a variety of negative characteristics such as laziness and sloppiness.[2] One potential consequence of such discrimination is that overweight children may choose as friends other children who are younger than they and who may be less inclined to discriminate, less judgmental about the older child's weight, or more eager to play with the overweight child because he or she is older.

Despite the negative connotations of obesity, overweight young children do not have a negative self-image or low self-esteem.[3, 4] However, obese adolescents develop a negative self-image that appears to persist into adulthood.[5] One explanation for this apparent discrepancy between children and adolescents is that self-image is derived from parental messages in young children and increasingly from the culture as children become adolescents.

The effect of psychosocial factors within the family on the origins of obesity and its psychosocial consequences has received limited attention in the United States. Several Swedish studies have demonstrated an association of parental neglect and obesity.[6] Furthermore, an increased prevalence of behavioral and learning difficulties has been observed among children who are gaining weight rapidly.[7] Whether learning difficulties reflect the subtle effects of sleep apnea or psychosocial problems within families requires additional studies. The psychological difficulties present in obese children may reflect maternal psychopathology or socioeconomic status (SES) rather than problems that result from the child's obesity.[8] Demonstration of the causal pathways that link obesity to psychosocial difficulties requires careful prospective studies.

EFFECT OF BODY SIZE ON SOCIALIZATION

Early maturation is associated with an increase in body fatness. Furthermore, children who mature early tend to have lower self-esteem.[9] To date, the effects of increased fatness on self-esteem have not been distinguished from the effects of early maturation. The effects of the two should be similar. White girls who develop a negative body image early in adolescence appear at greater risk for development of subsequent eating disorders.[10] No studies have examined these associations in other groups, such as black children.

The relationship of the effects of obesity in childhood on how adults relate to children and the consequent effects of such treatment on psychosocial development have not been examined carefully. As discussed in greater detail below, overweight children often are taller than their nonoverweight peers. Adults who do not know the age of overweight children often mistake them for older than their chronologic age and treat them accordingly. The expectation that a child can perform or converse at a level that is older than his or her chronologic age may lead to frustration on the part of the child or a sense of failure that such expectations cannot be fulfilled. No one has examined carefully the potential adverse effects of such treatment on the overweight child's capacity for interaction or socialization. One potential consequence is that the inadequacy the overweight child feels in response to inappropriate expectations of adults outside the family may lead the child to become less venturesome with respect to outside relationships with adults, increasingly dependent on family, and therefore increasingly isolated.

Social Consequences of Obesity in Young Adults Obese as Adolescents

At least one early study demonstrated that among girls who applied to an elite group of New England colleges, acceptance rates were lower among those who were overweight than among nonoverweight peers with comparable credentials.[11] The extent to which acceptance rates affect long-term achievement and income is not clear. Nonetheless, this study emphasizes the insidious expression of weight prejudice that is clearly operable when an overweight child reaches adolescence.

As early as 1960, Gam and Clark[12] demonstrated an association of obesity with SES. Among men, the relationship of obesity to SES was direct throughout the range of SES; in women, the association of SES with obesity was direct among young girls but inverse among women. Subsequent studies have replicated Gam and Clark's findings.[13] Because the early studies were cross-sectional, it was not possible to determine whether the inverse association between SES and obesity among women was a cause or a consequence of obesity.

The National Longitudinal Survey of Youth offered an opportunity to examine the effects of obesity in adolescence on social achievement in early adulthood.[14] The National Longitudinal Survey of Youth surveyed ~10 000 individuals 16 to 24 years of age. Among women who were obese in late adolescence and early adulthood, the number of years of advanced education completed, the family income, and the rates of marriage were significantly lower than rates among women who were not obese at the same ages. Furthermore, rates of poverty were higher. No such relationships were observed for men. The persistence of the effects of obesity on these areas of social performance, even when controlled for the income and education of the family of origin, suggested that obesity was a cause rather than a consequence of SES. Similar data have been published from a British cohort of 23-year-old men and women.[15] Interestingly, the magnitude of the effect of obesity on social indices was comparable.

Comparison of the performance of obese female adolescents and young adults with the performance of women with a variety of other chronic conditions demonstrated that only obesity exerted an adverse effect on these indicators.[14] These data suggest that obesity may be the worst socioeconomic handicap that women who were obese adolescents can suffer.

PREOCCUPATION WITH WEIGHT

In adults, eating disorders such as binge-eating disorder occur with increased prevalence among overweight women and substantially reduce the response to therapy.[16] The prevalence of eating disorders in children or adolescents has received less intensive investigation. Nonetheless, the available evidence suggests that both eating disorders and weight preoccupation exist among white children and adolescents, particularly females, and may impair the normal regulation of food intake.

For example, a cross-sectional study of 7- to 13-year-old children demonstrated that almost half were concerned about their weight, more than one third had already tried to lose weight, and almost one tenth manifested responses consistent with anorexia nervosa.[17] As expected, more girls than boys were preoccupied with weight, and concerns about weight increased with age. Few studies of ethnic differences in weight preoccupation have been performed. Although obese adult black women are less preoccupied with the social consequences of their obesity,[18] more black than white preadolescent girls are chronic dieters.[19]

Among older morbidly obese girls, unequivocal binge-eating disorder occurred in ~30% of patients,[20] which is comparable to the prevalence of binge-eating disorder among obese adult women.[16] However, the prevalence of binge-eating disorder among obese adolescents has not been compared with its prevalence in the nonobese adolescent population. Whether abnormal eating behaviors in adolescents affect the outcome of weight-reduction therapy remains unclear.

Few estimates of these behaviors have been made in the general population. Among almost 2000 adolescent high school students, disordered eating appeared to occur in ~2% of all students, but 11% of girls were classified as emotional eaters. Bingeing and feeling out of control about food were the principal abnormalities described.[21] The relationship of early abnormal eating behaviors to subsequent changes in body weight or to development of frank binge-eating disorders has not been studied carefully.

Psychosocial consequences represent the most prevalent morbidity associated with obesity. As indicated above, psychosocial effects may both contribute to and result from obesity. Longitudinal studies are essential to distinguish cause and effect. Furthermore, the effects of psychosocial difficulties of either parents or children on the outcome of therapy suggest that early identification and specific treatment for this subset of patients may be required. Despite the widespread preoccupation with weight and the concurrent increase in the prevalence of obesity, no studies of children have linked restrictive eating in preadolescents either to obesity or to eating disorders in adolescence or adulthood, or compared the prevalence of eating disorders in overweight and nonoverweight children or adolescents. Valid and reliable measures of eating behaviors are essential to clarify this problem.

Because greater acceptance of increased body weight exists among black women, and because eating disorders occur less frequently among black women and girls, additional studies of black females may help identify cultural norms that will lead to interventions that do not heighten concern about weight.

COMMON MEDICAL CONSEQUENCES OF OBESITY

Growth

Overweight children tend to be taller, have advanced bone ages, and mature earlier than nonoverweight children." Longitudinal studies of children who became overweight have shown that height gain accelerates or follows shortly after excessive weight gain.[22]

Early maturation, determined by bone age, peak height velocity, and age of menarche, is associated with increased fatness in adulthood[23, 24] as well as with an increase in the truncal distribution of fat in women.[25] In these studies, early maturation was associated with an increase in fatness at the same chronologic age, suggesting that those individuals who mature early were already fatter at the time maturation began. Nonetheless, even when it was adjusted for greater fatness at the same chronologic age, early maturation was still associated with increased fatness[24] in later life. As indicated above[10] early maturation also may increase the likelihood of eating disorders. However, in a study characterized by limited measurements, height velocity was not linked to subsequent mortality, although both prepubertal and postpubertal weights were related directly to death rates.[26]

These findings suggest that early maturation may represent an additional biologic determinant of obesity and perhaps its complications that operate at puberty. The determinants of the increased body fatness and the increased truncal deposition of fat remain uncertain. Furthermore, the long-term effects of early maturation on development of binge-eating disorder or on the comorbidity of obesity have not yet been evaluated carefully.

One of the most controversial suggestions was that the timing of menarche depended on a critical mass of body fat.[27] The suggestion that a critical level of fatness was necessary for both the onset and maintenance of menstruation provided an attractive explanation for the timing of the cessation and resumption of menses in women with anorexia nervosa before and after treatment.[28] The importance of a critical level of body fat for menstrual function was subsequently disputed.[29, 30] However, the recent observation that mice treated with leptin appear fertile earlier than untreated mice suggests that fatness may affect fertility through an effect on leptin concentrations.[31] Additional studies that link maturational timing, timing, leptin concentrations, and subsequent obesity may offer insights into the potential mechanisms that link these phenomena.

Hyperlipidemia

Increased blood lipids occur among obese children and adolescents. The characteristic pattern observed consists of elevated serum low-density lipoprotein (LDL)—cholesterol and triglycerides and lowered high-density lipoprotein-cholesterol levels.[32] Central fat distribution, perhaps through its effect on insulin levels, appears to be an important mediating variable between lipid levels and obesity.[33–36] Potential mechanisms are similar to those operative in adults. Increased free fatty acids produced by increased lipolysis by visceral adipocytes and hyperinsulinemia may promote hepatic triglyceride and LDL-cholesterol synthesis. Weight reduction clearly has a beneficial effect on these cardiovascular risk factors and may have a greater effect among girls with abdominal obesity.[37]

These studies, like those summarized below that have examined glucose and insulin metabolism, rarely have included simultaneous sophisticated measures of body composition and fat distribution. Instead, most studies have relied on skinfolds to calculate total body fat or on waist-to-hip ratios or extremity-to-trunk skinfold ratios as indices of fat distribution. However, neither waist-to-hip ratios nor skinfold ratios provide valid measures of intraabdominal fat.[38] The degree of imprecision associated with anthropometric estimates of total body or visceral fat is considerable and may confound many of the relationships sought. Misclassification or bias may produce spurious positive relationships, weaken significant associations, or lead to negative findings when significant associations exist. When visceral fat was measured directly by magnetic resonance imaging, an equally precise measure of body fat was not included.[32, 36] Therefore, the associations of morbidity with visceral fat may not be independent of total body fat. Because hyperhpidemia is common among overweight children and adolescents, a fasting lipoprotein profile should be obtained routinely.

Glucose Intolerance

Because obesity is tightly linked to diabetes in animal models of obesity, it is not surprising that glucose intolerance and diabetes are among the most frequent morbid effects of adult obesity.[39] Although few data are available about the frequency of glucose intolerance among obese children and adolescents, the recent observation that noninsulin-dependent diabetes mellitus (NIDDM) accounted for one third of all new cases of diabetes in Cincinnati in 1994[40] suggests that the morbid effects of the recent increases in the prevalence of, obesity have already begun. The incidence of NIDDM among adolescents in Cincinnati appears to have increased 10-fold since 1982. The mean body mass index (BMI) was 37 among the newly diagnosed NIDDM adolescent patients.

The mechanism by which obesity causes NIDDM in adolescents may be similar to that observed in adults. Visceral fat, measured by magnetic resonance imaging, appears related directly to basal insulin secretion, stimulated insulin secretion, and insulin resistance.[36] Unfortunately, in both this and other reports,[32, 37] total body fat and visceral fat have not been measured simultaneously. Therefore, it is impossible to determine whether visceral fat has an effect on insulin and glucose metabolism that is independent of the effects of total body fat. The association of insulin resistance with puberty and the deposition of visceral fat may identify puberty as a relevant period in which to examine causal linkages between adiposity, the behaviors that lead to fat deposition, and insulin resistance.

Acanthosis nigricans describes increased thickness and pigmentation of skin in intertriginous folds; it is associated with glucose intolerance in children and adolescents.[41] The prevalence of acanthosis nigricans among obese patients may be as high as 25%,[42] consistent with my own consecutive estimates from observations of 100 obese children.

Based on the contribution of obesity to diabetes in adults and the prevalence of acanthosis nigricans in overweight children and adolescents, measures of fasting insulin and glucose should be included routinely as part of the medical examination.

Hepatic Steatosis and Cholelithiasis

High concentrations of liver enzymes represent a frequent obesity-associated finding in children and adolescents. In a large Japanese series, [is less than] 10% of all obese children seen in a general obesity clinic setting had modest increases of liver enzymes, frequently associated with fatty liver, fatty hepatitis, fatty fibrosis, or cirrhosis.[43] Hyperinsulinemia also may play a role in the pathophysiology of steatohepatitis.[44] Weight reduction induces a normalization of hepatic enzymes.[45]

Cholelithiasis occurs with increased frequency among obese adults[46] and may occur even more frequently with weight reduction.[47] Increased cholesterol synthesis[48] and cholesterol saturation of bile[49] occurs in obesity. Although gallstones are a less frequent occurrence among obese children and adolescents, almost 50% of cases of cholecystitis in adolescents may be associated with obesity.[50] Furthermore, as in adults, cholecystitis in adolescents may be associated with weight reduction.[50]

LESS COMMON MEDICAL CONSEQUENCES OF OBESITY

Hypertension

Hypertension occurs with low frequency in children. In the best community-based study of this problem, only 1% of [is less than] 6600 school children 5 to 18 years of age had persistently elevated blood pressure.[51] However, almost 60% of the children with persistently elevated blood pressure had relative weights [is greater than] 120% of the median for their sex, height, and age. Based on the estimated prevalence of obesity in this sample,[52] persistently elevated blood pressure occurred approximately nine times more frequently among the obese. Correlations of childhood systolic pressure with systolic pressure observed in 26- to 30-year-olds ranged from $r = .27$ to $r = .39$; correlations of childhood diastolic pressure with adult diastolic pressure ranged from $r = .24$ to $r = 31$.[53] Childhood blood pressure and change in BMI were consistently the two most powerful predictors of adult blood pressure across all ages and both genders.[53] Although only limited follow-up is available regarding the long-term consequences of obesity-associated hypertension, substantial morbidity has been observed less than a decade after the original assessment, such as hypertensive heart disease or cerebral hemorrhage.[54]

Hypertension appears to be another consequence of hyperinsulinemia.[55–57] Hyperinsulinemia produces a significant decrease in renal sodium retention in both obese and nonobese adolescents,[58] and dietary therapy, particularly when it is accompanied by exercise, effectively decreases blood pressure.[59]

Pseudotumor Cerebri

Pseudotumor cerebri is a rare disorder of childhood and adolescence. The disease is characterized by increased intracranial pressure. Pseudotumor cerebri presents with headaches and may lead to severe visual impairment or blindness.[60] Papilledema usually occurs at some time during the course of the illness. Most cases occur before adolescence.[60, 61] Up to 50% of children who present with this syndrome may be obese, but the onset of symptoms does not appear to correlate with weight gain.[60] The potential for visual impairment indicates the need for aggressive treatment of obesity in patients with pseudotumor cerebri.

Sleep Apnea

Sleep apnea is another consequence of childhood obesity for which aggressive therapy is warranted. The only published estimate of the prevalence of sleep apnea among obese children and adolescents suggests that sleep apnea occurs in ~7% of obese children.[62] However, one third of children whose body weight was [is greater than] 150% of ideal body weight with a history of breathing difficulties during sleep were found to have apnea.[62] Neither the degree of obesity nor any question about a history of breathing difficulties during sleep predicted the severity of the obstruction. Neurocognitive deficits are common among obese children with sleep apnea.[63] In two of the more severe cases, a tonsillectomy and adenoidectomy in one case, and weight reduction in a second, improved the sleep apnea substantially. The relationship between sleep apnea and the obesity hypoventilation syndrome remains unclear. Hypoventilation may represent a long-term consequence as well as a cause of sleep apnea. The high mortality reported among published cases of the obesity hypoventuation syndrome[64] suggests that aggressive therapy is warranted for obese children with this syndrome.

Orthopedic Complications

Because the tensile strength of bone and cartilage did not evolve to carry substantial quantities of excess weight, a variety of orthopedic complications accompany childhood and adolescent obesity. Among young children, excess weight can lead to bowing of the tibia and femurs analogous to the bowing that occurs when downward pressure is exerted on a flexible stick. The resultant overgrowth of the medial aspect of the proximal tibial metaphysis is known as Blount disease. Although the prevalence of Blount disease is low, approximately two thirds of patients may be obese.[65] Slipped capital femoral epiphysis results from the effect of increased weight on the cartilaginous growth plate of the hip.[66] Between 30% and 50% of patients with slipped capital femoral epiphysis are overweight.[67, 68] Because Blount disease may recur and because there is increased risk for development of bilateral slipped capital femoral epiphysis if the other has already slipped, prompt and sustained weight reduction is essential.

Polycystic Ovary Disease (PCOD)

Among adult women who considered themselves normal and who had not sought treatment for menstrual irregularities, infertility, or hirsutism, 14% had polycystic ovaries diagnosed by ultrasonography.[69] Up to 30% of women with PCOD may be obese.[70] Hyperandrogenism and hyperinsulinemia frequently accompany the syndrome.[70, 71] Obesity is frequently associated with PCOD, but the pathophysiology is complex.[72, 73] Menstrual abnormalities may begin at adolescence.[74] An association of obesity, acanthosis nigricans, insulin resistance, and hyperandrogenemia has been identified in adolescent patients.[41]

The process of adolescent maturation appears ideally suited for the study of the relative contribution of body fatness, fat distribution, hyperandrogenemia, hyperinsulinemia, and PCOD. Nonetheless, most studies of this problem have been cross-sectional rather than longitudinal. Furthermore, the contribution of obesity and hyperinsulinemia in adolescents to the prevalence of PCOD in adults has not been evaluated definitively.

PERSISTENCE OF OBESITY AND ITS ASSOCIATED RISK FACTORS

Although critical periods appear to exist for the onset of obesity in childhood,[75] the relative contribution of obesity that begins in the prenatal period, the period of adiposity rebound, or in adolescence to the prevalence of adult obesity and its associated complications remains unclear. Odds ratios represent the most useful clinical expression of the likelihood that obesity will persist. In the Fels sample, the odds ratio for obesity at age 35 years increased from ~2 for males and females who were obese between the ages of 1 and 6 years to 5 to 10 for children who were obese at ages 10 to 14 years. The odds ratios for subsequent obesity at ages 15 to 18 years ranged from 8 to 57 for males and from 6 to 35 for females.[76] In other studies that tracked obesity, correlation coefficients have ranged from $r = .54$ to $.72$ depending on the group sampled.[77, 78] However, these correlation coefficients may be low because of the inclusion of a broad age range.[78] Among the studies that have examined the effects of childhood-onset obesity on adult obesity, at least one has shown that the prevalence of morbid obesity in adults appears to occur with a greater prevalence among individuals who were obese as adolescents.[79] However, only 15% to 30% of obesity in adults[80, 81] is a result of obesity that was present in childhood or adolescence.

Studies of the tracking of obesity have rarely examined the effect of the first incidence of obesity on the likelihood that it will persist. Several studies in progress should clarify this problem. However, the finding that there was an increased likelihood of persistence of obesity into adulthood among individuals who first became obese at the time of adiposity rebound or at adolescence suggests that this approach may clarify the relative contribution of obesity at different ages of onset to the prevalence of adult obesity and its consequences.

Few studies have examined the long-term effects of childhood or adolescent obesity on adult morbidity or mortality. One long-term follow-up study demonstrated that mortality was increased among men but not women who were obese during adolescence.[82] All-cause mortality, deaths from coronary heart disease, atherosclerotic cerebrovascular disease, and colon cancer were increased. Among both men and women, the occurrence of coronary heart disease, atherosclerosis, and diabetes was also increased. Colorectal cancer and gout were increased among men, and arthritis was increased among women. Because no increase in mortality has been attributed to growth rates per se,[23] these findings suggest that adolescent obesity rather than the rapid growth rates that accompany it may be responsible for the excess mortality in adulthood. However, the study cited[23] included relatively few growth points. Therefore, growth velocity throughout childhood and growth velocity at specific intervals in childhood still may act as a contributing factor.

The change in body fat that occurs in adolescence appears a reasonable mediator that entrains the excess morbidity and mortality that occurs in later adulthood among obese adolescents. In girls, adolescence represents a time of rapid fat accretion. Likewise, body fat redistributes from the periphery to a more central distribution in both sexes, although abdominal fat accumulation is more pronounced in males than in females. Therefore, the increases in body fat that occur in adolescent girls may be compounded by the development of obesity at this time. Among boys, the development of obesity during adolescence may predispose to increased visceral fat accumulation.

Multiple studies of children and adolescents have demonstrated clearly that systolic blood pressure, total and LDL-cholesterol, plasma insulin, and obesity tend to cluster.[83, 84] Furthermore, these variables tend to track with age. A high likelihood exists that cardiovascular risk factors present in obese children or adolescents will persist into young adulthood. Data from existing studies could be explored further to examine the relationship of age of onset to the development of later morbidity.

Several important problems remain. First, it is unclear whether the risk of obesity-associated morbidities varies with either the age of onset, severity of obesity, its duration, or factors responsible for its onset. Although early maturation appears related to the development of obesity at the period of adiposity rebound in both sexes and at the time of adolescence in girls, the biological or behavioral mechanisms that are responsible remain uncertain. Second, one long-term follow-up of individuals who were obese in adolescence demonstrated that the likelihood of cardiovascular disease appeared independent of the effect of adolescent obesity on adult weight status.[82] No long-term studies indicate that weight reduction after adolescence reduces the risk of adult morbidity. The development of the hyperinsulinemia that may constitute a pathophysiologic link between obesity and its several cardiovascular consequences remains unclear. As indicated previously, the independent effects of total body fat and visceral fat on cardiovascular risk have not been evaluated adequately. Furthermore, no prospective studies have linked the development of obesity and increased visceral adiposity to cardiovascular risk factors. Studies of this type appear to be essential.

CONCLUSION

Several of the obesity-associated morbidities in children and adolescents require urgent and aggressive therapy. Furthermore, as severely overweight children and adolescents become more common, the risks of weight-related complications in adulthood will increase. Nonetheless, no consensus exists to indicate how extreme overweight in children and adolescents should be treated.

Many of the complications associated with childhood and adolescent obesity would benefit from longitudinal studies to clarify cause and effect. These complications include psychosocial difficulties, eating disorders, and the effect of inappropriate expectations of obese children whose growth is increased. Longitudinal studies that include simultaneous measures of ethnicity, cardiovascular risk factors, visceral fat, and the factors that control the quantity and location of fat deposition throughout childhood and adolescence are essential to distinguish the effects of total and regional fat deposition on cardiovascular risk. The latter is particularly important to determine whether age of onset of obesity has differential effects on the persistence, morbidity, and mortality of obesity. The same studies might also help clarify the importance of a variety of behaviors that covary with obesity, such as smoking, alcohol use, or inactivity, and influence the central deposition of body fat independent of their influence on total body fat. Based on the studies performed to date, it is not clear whether obesity alone or the behaviors that generate obesity are more important determinants of obesity and its complications.

Finally, as more decisions about the allocation of resources are based on cost-effectiveness, outcome studies of the treatment of childhood and adolescent obesity that examine the effect of treatment on adult disease should be accorded a high priority. The outcome of greatest interest is weight adjusted for height. The success of therapy instituted at different ages among children with and without sequelae of obesity has not been evaluated. Most of the adverse effects of obesity are rare in children but common in adults. No study has yet examined the future morbidity of overweight children who lose weight and subsequently gain weight in adulthood. Whether obesity present in childhood or whether treatment of obesity in childhood independent of its effects on weight has an effect on health or psychosocial function therefore remains uncertain.

CRITICAL THINKING QUESTIONS

1. Compare and contrast some of the short-term and long-term consequences of obesity in children in terms of physical health and social/emotional health.
2. Summarize the findings regarding the persistence of obesity in children. What do you think are the implications of these findings related to the individual and to society?

REFERENCES

1. Richardson SA, Goodman N, Hastorf AH, Dombusch SM. Cultural uniformity in reaction to physical disabilities. *Am Soc Rev.* 1961;26: 241–247
2. Staffieri JR. A study of social stereotype of body image in children. *J Perspect Soc Psychol.* 1967;7:101–104
3. Kaplan KM, Wadden TA. Childhood obesity and self-esteem. *J Pediatr.* 1986;109:367–370
4. Sallade J. A comparison of the psychological adjustment of obese vs. non-obese children. *J Psychosom Res.* 1973;17:89–96
5. Stunkard A, Burt V. Obesity and the body image. II. Age at onset of disturbances in the body image. *Am J Psychiatry.* 1967;123:1443–1447
6. Lissau 1, Sorenson TIA. Parental neglect during childhood and increased risk of obesity in young adulthood. *Lancet.* 1994;343:324–327
7. Mellbin T, Vuille J-C. Further evidence of an association between psychosocial problems and increase in relative weight between 7 and 10 years of age. *Acta Pediatr Scand.* 1989;78:576–580
8. Epstein LH, Myers MD, Anderson K. The association of maternal psychopathology and family socioeconomic status with psychological problems in obese children. *Obesity Res.* 1996;4:65–74
9. Brooks-Gunn J. Antecedents and consequences of variations in girls' maturational timing. *J Adolesc Health Care.* 1988;9:365–373
10. Attie I, Brooks-Gunn J. Development of eating problems in adolescent girls: a longitudinal study. *Dev Psychol.* 1989;25:70–79

11. Canning H, Mayer J. Obesity—its possible effect on college acceptance. *N Engl J Med.* 1966;275:1172–1174
12. Gam SM, Clark DC. Nutrition, growth, development, and maturation: findings from the ten-state nutrition survey of 1968–1970. *Pediatrics.* 1975;56:306–319
13. Sobal J, Stunkard AJ. Socioeconomic status and obesity: a review of the literature. *Psychol Bull.* 1989;105:260–275
14. Gortmaker SL, Must A, Perrin JM, et al. Social and economic consequences of overweight in adolescence and young adulthood. *N Engl J Med.* 1993;329:1008–1012
15. Sargent JD, Blanchflower DC. Obesity and stature in adolescence and earnings in young adulthood. *Arch Pediatr Adolesc Med.* 1994;148: 681–687
16. Yanovski SZ. Binge eating disorder: current knowledge and future directions. *Obes Res.* 1993;1:306–324
17. Maloney MJ, McGuire J, Daniels SR, Specker B. Dieting behavior and eating attitudes in children. *Pediatrics.* 1989;84:482–489
18. Kumanyika S, Wilson JF, Guilford-Davenport M. Weight-related attitudes and behaviors of black women. *J Am Diet Assoc.* 1993;93:416–422
19. Sdireiber GB, Robins M, Striegel-Moore R, et al. Weight modification efforts reported by black and white preadolescent girls: National Heart Lung and Blood Institute Growth and Health Study. *Pediatrics.* 1996;98:63–70
20. Berkowitz R, Stunkard AJ, Stallings VA. Binge-eating disorder in obese adolescent girls. *Ann NY Acad Sci.* 1993;699:200–206
21. Kagan DM, Squires RL. Eating disorders among adolescents: patterns and prevalence. *Adolescence.* 1984;19:15–29
22. Forbes GB. Nutrition and growth. *J Pediatr.* 1977;91:40–42
23. Van Lenthe FJ, Kemper HCG, van Mecehelen W. Rapid maturation in adolescence results in greater obesity in adulthood: the Amsterdam Growth and Health study. *Am J Clin Nutr.* 1996;64:18–24
24. Gam SM, LaVelle M; Rosenberg KR, Hawthorne VM. Maturational timing as a factor in female fatness and obesity. *Am J Clin Nutr.* 1986; 43:879–883
25. Van Lenthe FJ, Kemper HCG, van Mecehelen W, et al. Biological maturation and the distribution of subcutaneous fat from adolescence into adulthood: the Amsterdam Growth and Health study. *Int J Obes.* 1996; 20:121–129
26. Nieto FJ, Szklo M, Comstock GW. Childhood weight and growth rate as predictors of adult mortality. *Am J Epidemiol.* 1992;136:201–213
27. Frisch R, Revelle R. Height and weight at menarche and a hypothesis of critical body weights and adolescent events. *Science.* 1970;169:397–399

28. Frisch R, McArthur JW. Menstrual cycles: fatness as a determinant of minimum weight for height necessary for their maintenance or onset. *Science.* 1974;185:949–951
29. Scott EC, Johnston FE. Critical fat, menarche, and the maintenance of menstrual cycles: a critical review. *J Adolesc Health Care.* 1982;2:249–260
30. Ellison PT. Skeletal growth, fatness, and menarcheal age: a comparison of two hypotheses. *Hum Biol.* 1982;54:269–281
31. Chehab FF, Mounzih K, Lu R, Lim ME. Early onset of reproductive function in normal female mice treated with leptin. *Science.* 1997;275: 88–90
32. Caprio S, Hyman LD, McCarthy S, et al. Fat distribution and cardiovascular risk factors in obese adolescent girls: importance of the intra-abdominal fat depot. *Am J Clin Nutr.* 1996;64:12–17
33. Freedman DS, Srinivasan SR, Burke GL, et al. Relation of body fat distribution to hyperinsulinemia in children and adolescents: the BogalusaHeart Study. *Am J Clin Nutr.* 1987;46:403–410
34. Freedman DS, Srinivasan SR, Harsha DW, et al. Relation of body fat patterning to lipid and lipoprotein concentrations in children and adolescents: the Bogalusa Heart Study. *Am J Clin Nutr.* 1989;50:930–939
35. Steinberger J, Moorehead C, Katch V, Rocchini AP. Relationship between insulin resistance and abnormal lipid Profile in obese adolescents. *J Pediatr.* 1995;126:690–695
36. Caprio S, Hyman LD, Limb C, et al. Central adiposity and its metabolic correlates in obese adolescent girls. *Am J Physiol.* 1995;269:E118–E126
37. Wabitsch M, Hauner H, Heinze E, et al. Body-fat distribution and changes in the atherogenic risk-factor profile in obese adolescent girls during weight reduction. *Am J Clin Nutr.* 1994;60:54–60
38. Goran MI, Kaskoun M, Shuman WP. Intra-abdominal adipose tissue in young children. *Int J Obes.* 1995;19:279–283
39. Chan JM, Rimm EB, Colditz GA, et al. Obesity, fat distribution, and weight gain as risk factors for clinical diabetes in men. *Diabetes Care.* 1994;17:961–969
40. Pinhas-Hamiel O, Dolan LM, Daniels SR, et al. Increased incidence of non-insulin-dependent diabetes mellitus among adolescents. *J Pediatr.* 1996;128:608–615
41. Richards GE, Cavallo A, Meyer WJ III, et al. Obesity, acanthosis nigricans, insulin resistance, and hyperandrogenemia: pediatric perspective and natural history. *J Pediatr.* 1985;107:893–897
42. Neptune H, Nigrin GA. Acanthosis nigricans and hyperinsulinemia: an underdiagnosed cause of obesity. *Pediatr Res.* 1994;35(2):104A
43. Kinugasa A, Tsunamoto K, Furukawa N, et al. Fatty liver and its fibrous changes found in simple obesity of children. *J Pediatr Gastroenterol Nutr.* 1984;3:408–414

44. Wanless IR, Bargman JM, Oreopoulos DC, Vas SI. Subcapsular steatonecrosis in response to peritoneal insulin delivery: a clue to the pathogenesis of steatonecrosis in obesity. *Modern Pathol.* 1989;2:69–74
45. Vajro P, Fontanella A, Perna C, et al. Persistent hyperaminotransferasemia resolving after weight reduction in obese children. *J Pediatr.* 1994;125:239–241
46. Maclure KM, Hayes KC, Colditz GA, et al. Weight, diet, and the risk of symptomatic gallstones in middle-aged women. *N Engl J Med,* 1989;321: 563–569
47. Liddle RA, Goldstein RB, Saxton J. Gallstone formation during weight-reduction dieting. *Arch Intern Med.* 1989;149:1750–1753
48. Screibman PH, Dell RB. Human adipocyte cholesterol. Concentration, localization, synthesis, and turnover. *J Clin Invest.* 1975;55:986–993
49. Bennion LJ, Grundy SM. Effects of obesity and caloric intake on biliary lipid metabolism in man. *J Clin Invest.* 1975;56:996–1011
50. Crichlow RW, Seltzer MH, Jannetta PJ. Cholecystitis in adolescents. *Dig Dis.* 1972;17:68–72
51. Rames LK, Clarke WR, Connor WE, et al. Normal blood pressures and the elevation of sustained blood pressure elevation in childhood: the Muscatine study. Pediatrics. 1978;61:245–251
52. Lauer RM, Connor WE, Leaverton PE, et al. Coronary heart disease risk factors in school children: the Muscatine study. *J Pediatr.* 1975;86; 697–706
53. Lauer RM, Clarke WR. Childhood risk factors for high adult blood pressure: the Muscatine study. *Pediatrics.* 1989;84:633–641
54. Heyden S, Bartel AG, Hames CG, McDonough JR. Elevated blood pressure levels in adolescents, Evans County, Georgia. *JAMA.* 1969;209: 1683–1689
55. DeFronzo RA. The effect of insulin on renal sodium metabolism. *Diabetologia.* 1981;21:165–171
56. Yudkin JS. Hypertension and non-insulin dependent diabetes. *Br Med J.* 1991;303:730–733
57. Jiang X, Srinivasan SR, Bao W, Berenson GS. Association of fasting insulin with blood pressure in young individuals. *Arch Intern Med.* 1993;153:323–328
58. Rocchini AP, Katch V, Kveselis D, et al. Insulin and renal sodium retention in obese adolescents. *Hypertension.* 1989;14:367–374
59. Rocchini AP, Katch V, Anderson J, et al. Blood pressure in obese adolescents: effect of weight loss. *Pediatrics.* 1988;82:16–23
60. Weisberg LA, Chutorian AM. Pseudotumor cerebri of childhood. *Am J Dis Child.* 1977;131:1243–1248

61. Grant DN. Benign intracranial hypertension; a review of 79 cases in infancy and childhood. *Arch Dis Child.* 1971;46:651–655
62. Mallory GB Jr, Fiser D, Jackson R. Sleep-associated breathing disorders in morbidly obese children and adolescents. *J Pediatr.* 1989;115:892–897
63. Rhodes SK. Shimoda KC, Waid LR, et al. Neurocognitive deficits in morbidly obese children with obstructive sleep apnea. *J Pediatr.* 1995; 127:741–744
64. Riley DJ, Santiago TV, Edelman NH. Complications of obesity-hypoventilation syndrome in childhood. *Am J Dis Child.* 1976;130: 671–674
65. Dietz WH jr, Gross WL, Kirkpatrick JA Jr. Blount disease (tibia vara): another skeletal disorder associated with childhood obesity. *J Pediatr.* 1982;101:735–737
66. Kelsey JL, Keggi KJ, Southwick WO. The incidence and distribution of slipped femoral epiphysis in Connecticut and southwestern United States. *J Bone Joint Surg.* 1970;52A:1203–1216
67. Sorenson KH. Slipped upper femoral epiphysis. Acta Orthop Scand. 1968;39:499–517
68. Kelsey JL, Acheson RM, Keggi KJ. The body build of patients with slipped femoral capital epiphysis. *Am J Dis Child.* 1972;124:276–281
69. Polson DW, Wadsworth J, Adams J, Franks S. Polycystic ovaries—a common finding in normal women. *Lancet.* 1988;1:870–872
70. Goldzieher JW, Green JA. The polycystic ovary. 1. Clinical and histologic features. *J Clin Endocrinol Metab.* 1962;22:325–328
71. Kahn CR, Flier JS, Bar RS, et al. The syndromes of insulin resistance and acanthosis nigricans. *N Engl J Med.* 1976;294:739–745
72. Franks S. Polycystic ovary syndrome. *N Engl J Med.* 1995;333:853–861
73. McKenna TJ. Pathogenesis and treatment of polycystic ovary syndrome. N Engl f Med. 1988;318:558–562
74. Yen SSC. The polycystic ovary syndrome. *Clin Endocrinol.* 1980;12: 177–207
75. Dietz WH. Critical periods in childhood for the development of obesity. *Am J Clin Nutr.* 1994;59:995–999
76. Guo SS, Roche AF, Chumlea WC, et al. The predictive value of childhood body mass index values for overweight at age 35 y. *Am J Clin Nutr.* 1994;59:810–819
77. DiPietro L, Mossberg H-O, Stunkard AJ. A 40-year history of overweight children in Stockholm: life-time overweight, morbidity, and mortality. *Int J Obes.* 1994;18:585–590
78. Freedman DS, Shear CL, Burke G, et al. Persistence of juvenile onset obesity over eight years: the Bogalusa Heart Study. *Am J Public Health.* 1987;77:588–592

79. Rimm IJ, Rimm AA. Association between juvenile onset obesity and severe adult obesity in 73,532 women. *Am J Public Health.* 1976,66: 479–481
80. Braddon FEM, Rodgers B, Wadsworth MEJ, Davies JMC. Onset of obesity in a 36 year birth cohort study. *Br Med J.* 1986;293:299–303
81. Abraham S, Nordsieck M. Relationship of excess weight in children and adults. *Public Health Rep.* 1960;75:263–273
82. Must A, Jacques PF, Dallal GE, et al. Long-term morbidity and mortality of overweight adolescents; a follow-up of the Harvard Growth Study of 1922 to 1935. *N Engl J Med.* 1992;327:1350–1355
83. Bao W, Srinivasan SR, Wattigney WA, Berenson GS. Persistence of multiple cardiovascular risk clustering related to Syndrome X from childhood to young adulthood. *Arch Intern Med.* 1994;154:1942–1847
84. Wattigney WA, Webber LS, Srinivasan SR, Berenson GS. The emergence of clinically abnormal levels of cardiovascular risk factor variables among young adults: the Bogalusa Heart Study. *Prev Med.* 1995;24: 617–626

12

Middle Childhood: Cognitive Development

Genetics and Intelligence (Genetics of Childhood Disorders, part 1)

Robert J. Sternberg and Elena L. Grigorenko

Several studies have been conducted to determine the association between genetics and intelligence. These studies have also analyzed variations on the conceptualizations of intelligence by ethnic group and the existence of performance-based definitions of intelligence. Results have demonstrated that creative and practical abilities are also important like intelligence. In addition, findings have shown the critical role supported by genes in the development of individual differences in IQ.

In 1905, Alfred Binet and Theodore Simon succeeded in creating a test that would distinguish children with behavior problems from children who were mentally retarded. The idea was to prevent children in France who had behavior problems from being consigned to the dust heap that in those days constituted the classrooms for the mentally retarded. The test proved successful in predicting academic performance beyond that of just those children at the lower

Journal of the American Academy of Child and Adolescent Psychiatry, April 1999, v38, i4, p486(3).

© 1999 Lippincott/Williams & Wilkins.

end of the ability spectrum, and a variant of Binet's test, the Stanford-Binet, soon came to figure prominently in the landscape of American schooling. Eventually, the Stanford-Binet was joined by other tests, including individual measures such as the Wechsler series, and group measures such as the Otis tests.

So successful were these tests that Edward Boring, a Harvard psychologist in the 1920s, proposed that intelligence is nothing more than what tests of intelligence measure. Some might dismiss Boring's definition as trivial or circular, but it reflects a major issue here in the United States and abroad about the nature and measurement of intelligence. To this day, many psychiatrists as well as psychologists view intelligence as essentially what the tests measure.

Increasingly solid evidence is emerging that what psychological tests measure is only a part of the entire portrait of what intelligence is. Over the next several months, aspects of the nature of intelligence and the contribution of genetic factors to intelligence will be reviewed in this column.

Investigators have studied implicit, or folk, theories of intelligence around the world. People's intuitive concepts of intelligence are much broader than the conceptions represented by the tests. A number of studies have asked lay people what they understand intelligence to be. Their responses have included factors such as practical problem-solving ability, verbal ability, and social competence. Although verbal ability is carefully measured by existing tests, social competence is generally not measured at all.

Conceptualizations of intelligence vary by ethnic group. In a study of various groups in California, for example, Latino parents emphasized social competence skills in their definitions of intelligence whereas Asian and Anglo parents emphasized cognitive competence skills. Teachers' conceptions of intelligence corresponded more to that of the Asian and Anglo parents. Not surprisingly, children in these groups did better in school, perhaps in part because of the match between their socialization and the expectations of the school.

Outside the United States, the departures from the test-based notion are even greater. In a study conducted in Taiwan, intelligence embraced not only conventional cognitive abilities, but also interpersonal competence (understanding of others), intrapersonal competence (understanding of self), intellectual self-assertion (knowing when to show one's intelligence), and intellectual self-effacement (knowing when not to show one's intelligence).

But implicit theories do not tell the whole story. Performance-based definitions of intelligence exist as well. At least 2 kinds of abilities appear to be relatively distinct from the kinds of abilities measured by conventional intelligence tests: creative abilities and practical abilities. In one series of studies on creative intellectual abilities, individuals were asked to write stories with unusual titles such as "2985," to draw artistic compositions on unusual topics such as "The earth from an insect's point of view," to create advertisements for boring products such as a brand of "bow ties," or to suggest solutions to problems such as that of how we would recognize extraterrestrial aliens among us seeking to escape detection. Performance on tasks such as these proved to be only weakly to moderately correlated with scores on conventional tests of intelligence.

There is even more evidence for the relative independence of practical intellectual abilities from IQ and related measures. Practical intellectual abilities reflect the ability to solve commonsense problems a person encounters in the world of work. In multiple studies of business managers, academic psychologists, sales people, teachers, and military leaders, scores on tests of practical intelligence do not correlate well with IQ. Nonetheless, practical intelligence predicts job performance as well as or better than IQ. In a study of children in Kenya, a test of practical intelligence involved children's using knowledge they had acquired on how to use natural herbal medicines to fight infections. In Kenya, this knowledge is highly adaptive. Significant negative correlations were found with conventional kinds of ability measures.

In another set of studies, a test for high school students was developed that measured traditional analytical abilities of the kinds found on conventional intelligence tests, but also tests of creative and practical abilities. This battery used both multiple-choice items and essay questions in the verbal, quantitative, and figural domains. Analytical, creative, and practical abilities were found to be relatively uncorrelated. The general ("*g*") factor so prevalent in conventional tests accounted for little of the variance in the results. Apparently, this factor appears only when the tests measure a fairly narrow range of abilities.

In summary, the evidence suggests there is more to intelligence than IQ. Creative and practical abilities matter as well as the more conventional analytical abilities. These abilities are relatively independent of analytical abilities, but they are measured minimally or not at all by conventional tests. We need to develop new, expanded tests to assess a broader range of intellectual abilities. Indeed, lack of adequate psychometric tools assessing other than g-related intellectual abilities is one of the main reasons why the conventional view of intelligence dominates the field.

The field of behavioral genetics of intelligence uses the old, g-related view of IQ. Virtually none of the new developments in the general theory of intelligence have penetrated the field. The argument here is that any instrument used in behavioral-genetic studies needs to be psychometrically solid, and there is nothing in the field that even approaches the psychometric properties of *g*-based tests. Correspondingly, behavioral geneticists still conceptualize the domain of cognitive abilities only as a *g*-championed hierarchy of abilities.

Given the absolute power of the psychometric theory of intelligence in behavioral-genetic studies of intelligence, it is not surprising that such studies support the *g* view of intelligence. It is remarkable, however, that since the consensus was reached a number of years ago that genetic variability explains about 50% of observed individual differences in general cognitive ability (with an upper boundary of about 80% obtained through direct estimates of heritability using relatives reared apart and a lower boundary of about 40% obtained through indirect estimates of heritability using relatives reared together), behavioral-genetic models have not changed to accommodate the new evidence accumulated in psychological theories of intelligence.

Even though the importance of genes in the development of individual differences in IQ has been unequivocally established, these influences account for only half of the variability. Moreover, much debate was generated by the publication of *The Bell Curve,* which unequivocally supported the *g* view and the argument that *g* is subject to substantial genetic impact. It is clear that the issues of the definition of intelligence, genetic influences, and validity and reliability of modern intelligence tests remain to be discussed.

To date, behavioral-genetic research addresses exclusively the etiology of *g*-based abilities. Whereas other areas of psychology have appreciated the diversity of human abilities, the field of behavioral genetics remains a dedicated soldier in the *g*-empire. Although the findings about the heritability of *g*-based abilities are reliable and conclusive, *g* appears to be only one of the letters of the alphabet of human abilities.

WEB SITES OF INTEREST

http://www.leaderu.com/ftissues/ft9502/nathanson.html
http://www.sciam.com/askexpert/biology/biology19.html
http://serendip.brynmawr.edu/Letter-NYtimes.html

ADDITIONAL READINGS

Herrnstein RJ, Murray C (1994), *The Bell Curve: Intelligence and Class Structure in American Life.* New York: Free Press

Okagaki L, Sternberg RJ (1993), *Parental beliefs and children's school performance.* Child Dev 64:36–56

Sternberg RJ (1997), *Successful Intelligence.* New York: Plume

Sternberg RJ, Grigorenko EL (1997), *Intelligence, Heredity, and Environment.* New York: Cambridge University Press

Dr. Sternberg is Professor, and Dr. Grigorenko is a postdoctoral fellow, Department of Psychology, Yale University, New Haven, CT.

CRITICAL THINKING QUESTIONS

1. Compare and contrast the major theoretical constructs of intelligence discussed in this article. Summarize those similarities and differences.
2. How might a parent be able to use this information to better understand their child? How might teachers use this information?
3. Two other types of intelligence are noted in this article; creative and practical intelligence. Describe each and identify how each of these might affect a child's ability to be successful in school and how it might affect his or her ability to function successfully in society.

13

Middle Childhood: Social and Emotional Development

School Refusal in Children and Adolescents: A Review of the Past 10 Years

Neville J. King and Gail A. Bernstein

Objective: To critically review the past 10 years of research on school refusal in children and adolescents.

Method: Literature on school refusal published from 1990 onward was reviewed following a systematic search of PsycINFO. The review focuses on definitional issues, epidemiology and school refusal identification, diagnostic considerations, family functioning, assessment, treatment, and follow-up studies.

Results: While definitional and conceptual issues are still evident, promising developments have occurred in relation to assessment and treatment practices and understanding of the family context of school refusal.

Conclusions: From a clinical viewpoint, school refusal cases require comprehensive assessment and treatment. Advances have been made in the treatment of school refusal.

Journal of the American Academy of Child and Adolescent Psychiatry, Feb 2001, v40, i2, p197.

© 2001 Lippincott/Williams & Wilkins.

However, additional controlled studies evaluating interventions for school refusal are needed. J. Am. Acad. Child Adolesc. Psychiatry, *2001, 40(2):197–205.*

In keeping with society's expectations concerning education and school attendance, most children attend school on a regular and voluntary basis. For some children, however, school attendance is so distressing emotionally that they have difficulty attending school, a problem that often results in prolonged absence from school (Burke and Silverman, 1987; King et al., 1995). It is not surprising that school refusal behavior nearly always causes much stress to parents and school personnel. A plethora of treatment approaches have been tried, but many are of questionable efficacy and acceptability (Blagg, 1987; Gullone and King, 1991). Fortunately, there have been significant developments over the past decade in relation to science-based assessment and treatment practices which should help in the early identification and sound management of school-refusing children (King et al., 2000; Ollendick and King, 1998).

DEFINITION

Similar to many other clinicians and researchers (e.g., Phelps et al., 1992), we define school refusal as difficulty attending school associated with emotional distress, especially anxiety and depression. While terms such as separation anxiety and school phobia are often used interchangeably with school refusal, we prefer the latter term because of its descriptive and comprehensive nature. Kearney and Silverman (1996, p. 345) recently defined school refusal behavior as "child-motivated refusal to attend school or difficulties remaining in school for an entire day." Such definitions include youths who are completely absent from school, who initially attend school but then leave during the school day, who go to school after having behavioral problems such as morning tantrums or psychosomatic complaints, and who display marked distress on school days and plead with their caregivers to allow them to remain home from school. However, debates continue in the literature as to whether or not the construct of school refusal should also include truancy, school attendance problems associated with antisocial behavior, and conduct problems (Lee and Miltenberger, 1996). Clearly, any reading and interpretation of published work on school refusal must take into account these definitional issues.

SERIOUSNESS

From a societal-legal viewpoint, it should be recalled that school attendance is mandated by law. Quite apart from legal considerations, however, school refusal behavior should be regarded as a serious problem because it usually poses significant and adverse consequences. School refusal is often associated with short-term sequelae including poor academic performance, family difficulties, and peer relationship problems (Last and Strauss, 1990; Naylor et al., 1994). In relation to educational outcomes, some researchers estimate that about half of school refusers underachieve academically (e.g., Chazan, 1962). Furthermore, if school refusal behavior and associated problems are not managed successfully in the community; hospitalization might be recommended for the child. Clearly, school refusal interferes with the child's social and educational development (Berg and Nursten, 1996). Long-term consequences may include fewer opportunities to attend facilities of higher education, employment problems, social difficulties, and increased risk for later psychiatric illness (Buitelaar et al., 1994; Flakierska-Praquin et al., 1997; Kearney and Albano, 2000a).

EPIDEMIOLOGY AND SCHOOL REFUSAL IDENTIFICATION

Recent reviewers have concluded that school refusal occurs in approximately 5% of all school-age children, although the rates of school absenteeism are much higher in some urban areas (cf., Burke and Silverman, 1987; Kearney and Roblek, 1997; King et al., 1995). Most studies suggest that school refusal tends to be equally common in boys and girls (e.g., Granell de Aldaz et al., 1984; Kennedy, 1965). School refusal can occur throughout the entire range of school years, but it appears there are major peaks at certain ages and certain transition points in the child's life. Ollendick and Mayer (1984) concluded that school refusal is more likely to occur between 5–6 years and 10–11 years of age. For most cases of school refusal, the socioeconomic status of the family is considerably mixed (Baker and Wills, 1978; Last and Strauss, 1990).

As well as examining the prevalence of school refusal, information is also needed on exactly what is happening in schools in relation to early identification, management, and referral. Stickney and Miltenberger's (1998) survey of 288 schools in North Dakota, which included elementary, junior high, and senior high schools, found that 75% of schools reported having a school refusal identification system in place. Principals were most frequently reported to be responsible for the identification of school refusal. Overall, 2.3% of students were identified as "school refusers" (included truants). Almost half presented with somatic complaints in the absence of a medical condition, an important finding from the viewpoint of early identification and treatment. School refusers were most commonly referred to a social worker and least frequently referred to a psychiatrist (see also Kearney and Beasley, 1994).

DIAGNOSTIC CONSIDERATIONS

Berg et al. (1993) conducted a comprehensive DSM-III-R diagnostic evaluation of 80 youths, aged 13 to 15 years, who failed to attend school for at least 40% of a school term without satisfactory excuse. It is important to note that the sample was drawn from the normal school population. School attendance problems were classified as truancy school refusal, or neither. Evaluations showed that half the youths with attendance problems had no psychiatric disorder, a third had a disruptive behavior disorder, and a fifth had an anxiety or mood disorder. In contrast, one tenth of a control group of youths without school attendance problems were found to suffer from these psychiatric disorders. On examining the relationship between type of school attendance problem and DSM-III-R disorder, the authors affirmed: "The well established connection between truancy and antisocial conduct, and between school refusal and anxiety symptoms that has been found to exist in selected samples (Hersov, 1960; Bools et al., 1990) was a lso evident in the normal school population" (Berg et al., 1993, p. 1199).

Last and Strauss (1990) conducted a major investigation of anxiety-based school refusal. The authors examined 63 school-refusing children and adolescents (aged 7–17 years) referred to an outpatient anxiety disorders clinic. According to DSM-III-R criteria, the most common primary diagnoses included separation anxiety disorder (38%), social phobia (30%), and simple phobia (22%). Less frequent diagnoses included panic disorder and posttraumatic stress disorder. Many children had multiple diagnoses, the most common comorbid diagnosis being overanxious disorder. Age-of-onset data revealed that separation anxiety occurs at a much earlier age (mean = 8.7 years) than either social phobia or simple phobia (means = 12.4 and 12.9 years, respectively). In examining maternal histories, the researchers found that mothers of the children with separation anxiety were more likely to have experienced school refusal themselves than were the mothers of the combined simple and social-phobic group. By contrast, the phobic subjec ts tended to show more severe school refusal as determined by symptom severity ratings of clinicians relative to the separation-anxious children. The authors concluded, "Results suggest that there are two primary diagnostic 'subgroups' of school refusers—separation anxious and phobic" (Last and Strauss, 1990, p. 31). More recently, Martin et al. (1999) demonstrated distinct family history patterns in these two subgroups. Parents of school refusers with separation anxiety disorder had increased prevalence rates of panic disorder and panic disorder and/or agoraphobia. Parents of school refusers with phobic disorders had increased prevalence rates of simple phobia and simple and/or social phobias.

Several diagnostic studies have examined the comorbidity of anxiety and depressive disorders in clinic samples of school-refusing children. Bernstein (1991) compared four groups of school refusers: an anxiety disorder-only group (separation anxiety disorder and/or overanxious disorder, n = 27), a depressive disorder-only group (major depressive disorder or dysthymia, n = 27), an anxiety and depressive disorder group (comorbid for anxiety and depression, n = 24), and a no-anxiety disorder or depressive disorder group (an absence of anxiety and depressive disorders, n = 18). The last group comprised mainly children with disruptive behavior disorders. Results showed that the group with comorbid anxiety and depression scored the highest on rating scales of anxiety and depression, with the no-anxiety or depression group scoring the lowest. In general, the anxiety-only and depression-only groups scored similarly, with scores that were intermediate between the other two groups. The findings suggest that the como rbidity of anxiety and depressive disorders is associated with more severe symptoms.

Borchardt et al. (1994) compared age- and gender-matched groups of inpatient (n = 28) and outpatient school refusers (n = 28). While the inpatient and outpatient groups did not differ significantly on prevalence of anxiety disorders (75% and 85%, respectively), they differed significantly on rate of major depression (86% and 46%, respectively). Inpatients were also more likely to have severe symptoms.

In an investigation of anxious/depressed adolescent school refusers (n = 44), Bernstein et al. (1997) reported that these teenagers frequently report moderate or severe somatic complaints. The most common somatic complaints were of the autonomic and gastrointestinal type. Although this study did not involve comparison groups, findings are consistent with the picture of substantial symptoms in anxious/depressed school-refusing youths.

From these diagnostic studies, it is clear that school refusal is complex, with variable presentations. Nonetheless, there appears to be support for three primary, distinguishable clinical groups of school refusers: phobic school refusers, separation-anxious school refusers, and anxious/depressed school refusers. Other minor groups of school refusers include children who might be characterized by other anxiety disorders. However, somewhat different trends are evident among non–clinic-referred youngsters with school refusal. A much larger proportion of these school refusers do not meet criteria for a diagnosis (Berg et al., 1993), compared with clinic samples. Given the possible size of this group, it is hoped that such children will be examined more fully in future years.

Although the relationship between school refusal and psychiatric disorders has been extensively investigated, the role of learning or language disorders has received scant attention. This is surprising because developmental learning or language disorders cause significant frustration in the school setting and may predispose the vulnerable child or youth to school avoidance. Naylor and colleagues (1994) found school-refusing depressed adolescents on an inpatient psychiatric unit to have significantly more learning disabilities and language impairments compared with matched psychiatric controls. Hence, the researchers concluded that "academic and communicative frustration and the adolescent's resulting inability to meet the academic and social demands in the school environment may play a role in the etiology of school refusal" (Naylor et al., 1994, p. 1331).

FAMILY FUNCTIONING

Problematic family functioning has been highlighted as contributing to school refusal in children and adolescents (Hersov, 1985; Waldron et al., 1975). Yet only a few studies systematically evaluate school refusal families with instruments designed to measure family functioning (Bernstein et al., 1990a, 1999;

Bernstein and Borchardt, 1996; Kearney and Silverman, 1995). These studies describe several different patterns of family functioning in school refusal families. The work of Kearney and Silverman (1995) is unique because it identifies family subtypes (i.e., the enmeshed family, the conflictive family, the isolated family, the detached family, and the healthy family) which are supported by scores on the Family Environment Scale (FES) (Moos and Moos, 1986).

The FES was completed by 64 parents of children with school refusal (Kearney and Silverman, 1995). Supporting the concept of the enmeshed family subtype, families with a school-refusing child scored significantly lower than normative families on the Independence subscale of the FES. Approximately one third of families had less than a standard score of 40 on this subscale. With respect to the conflictive family subtype, parents of school refusers reported significantly higher scores than normative families on the Conflict subscale. Isolated families are depicted as families who do not participate in activities outside the family. In their sample, 28.1% of the families scored 40 or less on the FES Intellectual-Cultural Orientation subscale and 31.3% scored 40 or less on the FES Active-Recreational Orientation subscale. The researchers commented that isolated families may not seek or follow through with treatment for school refusal. Finally, healthy family profiles were found in 39.1% of the sample as defined by scores of 60 or more on the FES Cohesion or Expressiveness subscales, with either score more than the Conflict score. Kearney and Silverman (1995) did not present FES data to support the detached family subtype. Mixed profiles are also described—for example, school refusal families with characteristics of both enmeshment and conflict.

Bernstein et al. (1990b) used the Family Assessment Measure (FAM) (Skinner et al., 1983) in evaluating 76 school refusal families. Family functioning difficulties were identified on the Role Performance and Values and Norms subscales of the FAM. Difficulties with role performance suggest lack of agreement among family members regarding roles and trouble adapting to new roles (Steinhauer et al., 1984). Elevation on the Values and Norms subscale indicates inconsistency of family rules and differences between the family's values and those of the culture and subcultures wherein the family resides (Steinhauer et al., 1984). Four diagnostic groups of school-refusing children were evaluated: those with anxiety disorders only, those with depressive disorders only, those with comorbid anxiety and depressive disorders, and those with no anxiety or depressive disorders (primarily disruptive behavior disorders). Significantly fewer family functioning difficulties were found in families in which the child met criteria fo r anxiety disorder only compared with families in the other diagnostic categories.

In a sample of 134 families with school-refusing children, the FAM was used to evaluate the relationship between family constellation (mother-only versus intact family) and family functioning (Bernstein and Borchardt, 1996). Single-parent families (39.6%) were overrepresented in the sample compared with the general population. Significantly more difficulties on the FAM in the areas of role performance and communication were reported by mothers of school refusers in single-parent families compared with mothers of school refusers in families with two biological parents. Communication difficulties as measured on the FAM suggest inadequate or unclear communication within the family (Steinhauer et al., 1984).

Focusing on school refusers with comorbid anxiety disorders and major depression, Bernstein et al. (1999) assessed family functioning with the Family Adaptability and Cohesion Evaluation Scale II (FACES II) (Olson et al., 1982). The FACES II has been found to have good reliability (Olson et al., 1983) and validity (Hampson et al., 1991). The sample included 46 adolescents aged 12 to 18 years and their parents who completed the FACES II independently at the beginning of a treatment study of school refusal. The FACES II assesses adaptability and cohesion dimensions and family type (balanced, midrange, and extreme). Adolescents and parents viewed their families as rigid on the adaptability dimension and disengaged on the cohesion dimension. Combining adaptability and cohesion scores to establish the family type, 50% of teenagers, 38% of fathers, and 24% of mothers described their families as the extreme type.

These studies highlight several patterns of problematic family interactions that are present in school refusal families and likely contribute to the children refusing to go to school. Treatment of youths with anxiety disorders usually involves a multimodal approach which may include family therapy (American Academy of Child and Adolescent Psychiatry [AACAP], 1997). Targeting family dynamic difficulties is essential in successfully treating school refusal.

ASSESSMENT

To date, the AACAP has not published guidelines specifically on the assessment and treatment of children with school refusal. However, the "Practice Parameters for the Assessment and Treatment of Children and Adolescents With Anxiety Disorders" (AACAP, 1997) is particularly useful in the clinical management of many school refusal cases. This, of course, reflects the overlap between anxiety and school refusal.

School-refusing children and adolescents vary widely regarding their clinical presentation, family dynamics, and school situation. To meet this challenge it is recommended that assessment be multimethod and multi-informant. In addition to a clinical interview, comprehensive evaluation may include a semi-structured diagnostic interview; evaluation of factors maintaining the school refusal behaviors; ratings of severity of anxiety and depression from selfreport, parent, clinician, and teacher perspectives; assessment of family functioning; psychoeducational and language assessment; and review of school attendance.

Semistructured diagnostic interviews, such as the Anxiety Disorders Interview Schedule for DSM-IV: Child Version (ADIS for DSM-IV:C), can be useful in diagnostic evaluation (Silverman and Albano, 1996). The ADIS for DSM-IV:C involves separate child and parent interviews, with the time frame of the examination being the past year. The interviews, which are organized around diagnostic categories, permit differential diagnosis among major DSM disorders. Acceptable reliability and validity have been reported by researchers using this particular diagnostic instrument (e.g., Rapee et al., 1994; Silverman and Rabian, 1995).

Assessment should also determine the specific factors responsible for the maintenance of the child's school attendance difficulties. Now an important clinical tool, the School Refusal Assessment Scale (SRAS) (Kearney and Silverman, 1990, 1993) provides useful information on the extent to which children refuse school by virtue of negative and positive reinforcement. As well as being completed by the child, the SRAS has versions for parents and teachers, thus allowing for comparison of different informant perspectives. Although further research is needed on psychometric properties, empirical findings thus far are encouraging for interrater and test-retest reliability and concurrent validity (Daleiden et al., 1999; Kearney and Silverman, 1990, 1993).

The SRAS assesses four primary hypothesized maintaining variables, or functional conditions, including avoidance of stimuli that provoke negative affectivity (e.g., fear, anxiety, depression), escape from aversive social or evaluative situations (e.g., class presentations, groups of peers), attention-getting behavior or traditional separation anxiety (e.g., tantrums to obtain parental attention), and positive tangible rewards such as staying home to watch television (Kearney and Silverman, 1990, 1993, 1999).

Moreover, prescribed treatments are indicated for each of the functional conditions identified by the SRAS (Kearney and Albano, 2000a, b; Kearney and Silverman, 1990, 1993, 1999). A cognitive-behavioral therapy (CBT) manual for therapists (Kearney and Albano, 2000a) and a workbook for parents (Kearney and Albano, 2000b) are available which outline prescriptive treatments for school refusal. CBT techniques are described which target symptoms related to one of four primary maintaining variables associated with refusing school. For example, exposure/systematic desensitization is indicated for children with specific fears or phobias as in the first functional category. While case studies support the efficacy of this prescriptive approach (e.g., Chorpita et al., 1996), systematic investigation of treatment efficacy is planned (Albano, personal communication, 2000).

Recently, Heyne et al. (1998) reported the development and psychometric evaluation of an instrument for assessing the efficacy expectations of school-refusing children, the Self-Efficacy Questionnaire for School Situations (SEQ-SS). This instrument is the first to provide a standardized assessment of the child's perceptions regarding his or her ability to cope with potentially anxiety-provoking situations such as doing school work, handling questions about absence from school, and being separated from parents during school time. Factor analysis yielded two factors labeled academic/social stress and separation/discipline stress. The instrument has good internal consistency and high test-retest reliability with school-refusing children, but more empirical evaluation is required.

The Visual Analogue Scale for Anxiety-Revised (VAA-R) (Bernstein and Garfinkel, 1992) is a self-report instrument designed for the assessment of anxiety in school-refusing children. A psychometric evaluation of the VAA-R was undertaken with a clinic sample of school-refusing children (N = 86) and a community sample (N = 918). The authors found good reliability (internal consistency and test-retest reliability over 1 week) and concurrent validity. Factor analysis of VAA-R items identified three clinically meaningful factors: anticipatory/separation anxiety, performance anxiety, and affective response to anxiety. The VAA-R may be useful in identifying specific anxiety-producing situations such as being called on by the teacher or riding the school bus. Such information is helpful in the design of individualized school reentry programs.

Newer instruments with good psychometric properties for assessment of anxiety in children and adolescents include (1) self-report instruments—the Multidimensional Anxiety Scale for Children (March et al., 1997), the Screen for Child Anxiety Related Emotional Disorders (Birmaher et al., 1997), and the Spence Children's Anxiety Scale (Spence, 1997); and (2) a clinician rating scale—the Pediatric Anxiety Rating Scale (Riddle, personal communication, 2000). There have been significant advances in terms of clinically useful and empirically sound tools for the diagnosis and assessment of school-refusing children (see also Greenhill et al., 1998; Ollendick and King, 1998).

TREATMENT

The AACAP (1997) recommends a multimodal treatment plan for children with anxiety disorders. Consideration should be given to the following components: education and consultation, behavioral (exposure/return to school) or cognitive-behavioral strategies, family interventions, and pharmacological interventions if warranted by severity of symptoms (AACAP, 1997). Although sometimes suggested by parents and others, homebound tutoring is generally contraindicated. Our literature search revealed that research on treatment efficacy over the past decade has been mainly confined to CBT and pharmacotherapy.

Cognitive-Behavioral Therapy

Three major treatment evaluations support the efficacy of behavioral intervention or CBT for school refusal (Blagg and Yule, 1984; King et al., 1998; Last et al., 1998), although it should be noted that randomization to groups did not occur in the first trial (Blagg and Yule, 1984). The King et al. (1998) trial involved 34 school refusers, aged 5 to 15 years, who experienced recalcitrant school attendance problems and emotional distress. Diagnostic examination revealed that most (85%) experienced a current anxiety or phobic disorder. Families were randomly assigned to either a 4-week cognitive-behavioral intervention (six sessions with the child, five with the parents, and one with the teacher) or a waiting-list control condition. The manual-based intervention emphasized coping skills training, exposure (return to school), and contingency management at home and school.

Relative to waiting-list controls, children who received therapy exhibited a clinically significant improvement in school attendance—nearly all attained 90% or more school attendance. Treated children also underwent improvements on self-reports of fear, anxiety, and depression. At the same time the children developed confidence in their ability to cope with anxiety-provoking situations, such as parental separation or being teased by peers, as measured by the SEQSS. Parent report data provided further confirmation of the beneficial effects of treatment with reports of improvements for internalizing problems. Clinician ratings of global functioning also corroborated the improvements in school attendance, child self-report and parent report. As well as being efficacious on outcome measures, children and caregivers expressed high levels of "consumer satisfaction" with the flexibly implemented protocol. Maintenance of therapeutic gains was demonstrated at 3-month follow-up.

An important clinical and research question is the extent to which treatment improvements might be due to nonspecific aspects of intervention such as expectations of improvement, having a supportive therapist, and education about the problem. In the Last et al. (1998) study, all children had an anxiety disorder diagnosis and at least 10% absenteeism from classes for at least 1 month prior to participation in the study. Fifty-six school refusers were randomly assigned to 12 weekly sessions of CBT or educational support therapy. The CBT condition consisted of graduated in vivo exposure, cognitive restructuring, and coping self-statement training. Educational support therapy was included as an attention-placebo control condition; it involved a combination of educational presentations, supportive psychotherapy, and a daily diary for recording of thoughts and fears. Unlike CBT, therapists refrained from encouraging children to confront their fears or teaching them how to modify their thoughts. To ensure treatment fidelity, therapists followed specific manuals in each of the conditions.

Contrary to expectations, findings revealed no differences between CBT and educational support therapy. At posttreatment, both groups showed improvements on a variety of measures including school attendance, global improvement ratings, and self-reported anxiety and depression. There were also marked improvements in diagnostic caseness for both groups: 65% of the CBT completers and 50% of the educational support therapy completers no longer met diagnostic criteria for an anxiety disorder at posttreatment. In relation to predictors of treatment success, younger children and children with higher baseline school attendance levels showed the greatest improvement during therapy. A 4-week followup on school attendance showed that the majority of children who improved during therapy maintained treatment gains or continued to show improvement; there were no significant differences between the two groups. However, some children are not adequately treated with 12 weeks of CBT as demonstrated by the observation that 35% of subjects randomly assigned to CBT did not achieve 95% attendance after treatment. Furthermore, 60% of CBT completers had difficulty reentering school the following year (half of these subjects had moderate to extreme difficulty). This highlights the need to study duration of CBT treatment and whether booster sessions are helpful in maintaining therapy gains.

Pharmacotherapy

Four double-blind, placebo-controlled studies which evaluated the efficacy of tricyclic antidepressants in the treatment of anxiety-based school refusal showed conflicting results (Berney et al., 1981; Bernstein et al., 1990a; Gittelman-Klein and Klein, 1971, 1973; Klein et al., 1992). Small sample sizes, differences in comorbidity patterns, lack of control of adjunctive therapies, and differences in medication dosages explain the inconclusive findings.

Generally, medications are considered as part of a multimodal treatment plan for children and adolescents with anxiety disorders and are not prescribed alone, without concurrent therapy (AACAP, 1997). In an investigation of a multimodal treatment for school refusal, Bernstein and colleagues (2000) compared 8 weeks of the tricyclic antidepressant imipramine versus 8 weeks of placebo, each in combination with CBT for 63 school-refusing adolescents with comorbid anxiety and major depressive disorders. While anxiety and depressive symptoms improved for both groups, depression improved at a significantly faster rate in the imipramine group. Attendance (measured in hours of school attended per week) improved significantly for the imipramine group, but not for the placebo group. Using 75% school attendance as a definition of remission at the end of the study, 54.2% of the imipramine group met the criterion compared with only 16.7% of the placebo group. The low response rate with placebo plus CBT is likely explained by the fact that school refusers with comorbid anxiety disorder and major depression have the most severe symptoms (Bernstein, 1991). Thus, anxious/depressed school refusers require a multimodal treatment approach (medication plus CBT).

The selective serotonin reuptake inhibitors (SSRIs) are emerging as the initial choice for treating anxiety disorders in children and adolescents (Velosa and Riddle, 2000). Three open-label studies (Birmaher et al., 1994; Dummit et al., 1996; Fairbanks et al., 1997) and a small double-blind, placebo-controlled study (Black and Uhde, 1994) indicate that fluoxetine is beneficial in treating children and adolescents with anxiety disorders. Findings from a randomized, controlled clinical trial of 8 weeks of fluvoxamine (up to 300 mg/day) versus placebo for 128 children and adolescents with generalized anxiety disorder, separation anxiety disorder, or social phobia showed benefit with fluvoxamine (Research Units of Pediatric Psychopharmacology Anxiety Study Group, 2000). In the fluvoxamine group, 76% had a Clinical Global Impressions score of much improved or better compared with only 29% on placebo.

In addition, a randomized, double-blind study demonstrated 8 weeks of fluoxetine to be more efficacious than 8 weeks of placebo in treating 96 children and adolescents with major depression (Emslie et al., 1997). Since school refusers may present as phobic, separation-anxious, or anxious/depressed individuals, SSRIs are commonly selected to target their symptoms.

Benzodiazepines may be considered on a short-term basis, alone or in combination with an SSRI or tricyclic antidepressant, for a child with severe school refusal. Inasmuch as it may take several weeks to appreciate the benefits of an antidepressant, a benzodiazepine can be started simultaneously to alleviate acute anxiety symptoms until the effects of the antidepressant are apparent. Benzodiazepines are beneficial in targeting acute anxiety associated with medical procedures in children, as shown in an open-label (Pfefferbaum et al., 1987) and a double-blind, placebo-controlled study (Hennes et al., 1990). Data regarding dependence on benzodiazepines in children and adolescents are not available (Velosa and Riddle, 2000). Nonetheless, because of the theoretical possibility of dependence, benzodiazepines should be used for a period of several weeks instead of months (Riddle et al., 1999).

Follow-Up Studies

Despite their obvious importance, few follow-up studies of children with school refusal have been reported. Relying mainly on register data, Flakierska and her colleagues conducted two controlled follow-up investigations of the same sample of school refusers who received inpatient or outpatient treatment in Sweden (Flakierska et al., 1988; Flakierska-Praquin et al., 1997). In the second of these studies, the follow-up interval was 20 to 29 years, with subjects being older than 30 years. The original sample was confined to school refusers seen at ages 7 to 12 years, whose chart histories met DSM-III criteria for separation anxiety disorder (n = 35). These children were compared with age- and sex-matched non–school-refusing child psychiatric patients (n = 35) and a sample from the general population (n = 35) on a series of outcome measures. The investigation revealed that the school refusal cases had more psychiatric consultation and lived with their parents more often than the general population group and ha d fewer children than both comparison groups. These findings suggest that many separation anxious school refusers continue to have problems as adults and signal the need for follow-up interviews to ascertain more detailed information about their difficulties.

Naturalistic follow-up of anxious/depressed adolescents in the 8-week study of imipramine versus placebo in combination with CBT (Bernstein et al., 2000) revealed high utilization of mental health services after subjects completed the study (Bernstein et al., 2001). In the year after the study, two thirds of the follow-up sample received at least one psychotropic medication trial and three fourths had outpatient therapy. Despite these interventions, half of the follow-up sample met criteria for an anxiety disorder and a third had a depressive disorder at follow-up. This confirms the severity of symptoms in anxious/depressed adolescents and underscores the need to define optimal type and duration of acute and maintenance interventions.

CONCLUSIONS

This review revealed exciting advances in the field of school refusal over the past 10 years. A range of useful diagnostic and assessment tools are now available to clinicians, and there have been noteworthy advances in manual-based, flexible intervention packages. Resource materials such as manuals and clinician guidelines have been published on the cognitive-behavioral assessment and treatment of school-refusing children (Kearney and Albano, 2000a,b; King et al., 1995). The heterogeneity of school refusal and varied family dynamics speak to the need for continuing research efforts on the assessment-treatment interface. Finally, recent findings of follow-up investigations serve as a sobering reminder of the need to define duration of acute treatment and to evaluate maintenance treatments in order to develop interventions with longlasting effectiveness for school-refusing children and their families.

Dr. King is Associate Professor, Faculty of Education. Monash University, Victoria, Australia, Dr. Bernstein is Associate Professor and Director, Division of Child and Adolecent Psychiatry, University of Minnesota Medical School, Minneapolis.

Correspondence to Dr. King, Faculty of Education, Monash University, Clayton, Victoria 3168, Australia; e-mail: neville.king@tducaeion.

CRITICAL THINKING QUESTIONS

1. How is school refusal diagnosed and what do you think are the most critical causes of school refusal?
2. Who do you think should be involved in the treatment of a child who is refusing to go to school?
3. How do you think a parent could use this information to better understand and treat his or her child who is refusing to go to school?
4. What do you think might be the long-term consequences of school refusal?

REFERENCES

American Academy of Child and Adolescent Psychiatry (1997), Practice parameters for the assessment and treatment of children and adolescents with anxiety disorders. *J Am Acad Child Adolesc Psychiatry* 36(suppl):69S–84S

Baker H, Wills U (1978), School phobia: classification and treatment. *Br J Psychiatry* 132:429–499

Berg I, Butler A, Franklin J, Hayes H, Lucas C, Sims R (1993), DSM-II-R disorders, social factors and management of school attendance problems in the normal population. *J Child Psychol Psychiatry* 34:1187–1203

Berg I, Nursten J, eds (1996), *Unwillingly to School,* 4th ed. London: Gaskell

Berney T, Kolvin I, Bhate SR et al. (1981), School phobia: a therapeutic trial with clomipramine and short-term outcome. *Br J Psychiatry* 138:110–118

Bernstein G (1991), Comorbidity and severity of anxiety and depressive disorders in a clinic sample. *J Am Acad Child Adolesc Psychiatry* 30:43–50

Bernstein GA, Borchardt CM (1996), School refusal: family constellation and family functioning. *J Anxiety Disord* 10:1–19

Bernstein [*] GA, Borchardt CM, Perwien AR et al. (2000), Imipramine plus cognitive-behavioral therapy in the treatment of school refusal. *J Am Acad Child Adolesc Psychiatry* 39:276–283

Bernstein GA, Garfinkel BD (1992), The Visual Analogue Scale for Anxiety-Revised: psychometric properties. *J Anxiety Disord* 6:223–239

Bernstein GA, Garfinkel BD, Borchardt CM (1990a), Comparative studies of pharmacotherapy for school refusal, *J Am Acad Child Adolesc Psychiatry* 29:773–781

Bernstein GA, Hektner JM, Borchardt CM, McMillan MH (2001), Treatment of school refusal: one-year follow-up. *J Am Acad Child Adolesc Psychiatry* 40:206–213

Bernstein GA, Massie ED, Thuras PD, Perwien AR, Borchadt CM, Crosby RD (1997), Somatic symptoms in anxious-depressed school refusers. *J Am Acad Child Adolesc Psychiatry* 36:661–668

Bernstein GA, Svingen P, Garfinkel BD (1990b), School phobia: patterns of family funceioning. *J Am Acad Child Adolesc Psychiatry* 29:24–30

Bernstein GA, Warren SL, Massie ED, Thuras PD (1999), Family dimensions in anxious-depressed school refusers. *J Anxiety Disord* 13:513–528

Birmaher B, Khetalarpal S, Brent D et al. (1997), The Screen for Child Anxiety Related Emotional Disorders (SCARED): scale construction and psychometric characteristics. *J Am Acad Child Adolesc Psychiatry* 36:545–553

Birmaher B, Waterman GS, Ryan N et al. (1994), Fluoxetine for childhood anxiety disorders. *J Am Acad Child Adolesc Psychiatry* 33:993–999

Black B, Uhde TW (1994), Treatment of elective mutism with fluoxetine: a double blind placebo study. *J Am Acad Child Adolesc Psychiatry* 33:1000–1006

Blagg N (1987), *School Phobia and its Treatment.* London: Croom Helm

Blagg N, Yule W (1984), The behavioural treatment of school refusal: acomparative study. *Behav Res Ther* 22:119–127

Bools C, Foster J, Brown I, Berg I(1990), The identification of psychiatric disorders in children who fail to attend school: a cluster analysis of a non-clinical population. *Psychol Med* 20: 171–178

Borchardt CM, Giesler J, Bernstein GA, Crosby RD (1994), A comparison of inpatient and outpatient school refusers. *Child Psychol Hum Dev* 24:255–264

Buitelaar JK, van Andel H, Duyx JHM, van Strien DC (1994), Depressive and anxiety disorders in adolescence: a follow-up study of adolescents with school refusal. *Acta Paedopsychiatr* 56:249–253

Burke AE, Silverman WK (1987), The prescriptive treatment of school refusal. *Clin Psychol Rev* 7:353–362

Chazan M (1962), School phobia. *Br J Educ Psychol* 32:201–207

Chorpita BF, Albano AM, Heimberg RG, Barlow DH (1996), A systematic replication of the prescriptive treatment of school refusal behavior in a single subject. *J Behav Ther Exp Psychiatry* 27:28 1–290

Daleiden EL, Chorpita BF, Kollins SC, Drabman RS (1999), Factors affecting the reliability of clinical judgements about the function of school-refusal behavior. *Child Psychol* 28:396–406

Dummit ES, Klein RG, Tancer NK, Asche B, Martin J (1996), Fluoxetine treatment of children with selective mutism: an open trial. *J Am Acad Child Adolest Psychiatry* 35:615–621

Emslie GJ, Rush J, Weinberg WA et al. (1997), A double blind, randomized, placebo-controlled trial of fluoxetine in children and adolescents with depression. *Arch Gen Psychiatry* 54:1031–1037

Fairbanks JM, Pine DS, Tancer NK et al. (1997), Open fluoxetine treatment of mixed anxiety disorders in children and adolescents. *J Child Adolesc Psychopharmacol* 7:17–29

Flakierska, N, Lindstrom M, Gillberg C (1988), School refusal: a 15–20-year follow-up study of 35 Swedish urban children. *Br J Psychiatry* 152:834–837

Flakierska-Praquin N, Lindstrom M, Gillberg C (1997), School phobia with separation anxiety disorder: a comparative 20- to 29-year follow-up of 35 school refusers. *Comp Psychiatry* 38:17–22

Gittelman-Klein R, Klein DF (1971), Controlled imipramine treatment of school phobia. *Arch Gen Psychiatry* 25:204–207

Gittelman-Klein R, Klein DF (1973), School phobia: diagnostic considerations in the light of imipramine effects. *J Nerv Ment Dis* 156:199–215

Granell de Aldaz E, Vivas E, Gelfand DM, Feldman L (1984), Estimating the prevalence of school refusal and school-related fears: a Venezuelan sample. *J Nerv Ment Dis* 172:722–729

Greenhill LL, Pine D, March J, Birmhaher B, Riddle M (1998), Assessment measures in anxiety disorders research. *Psychopharmacol Bull* 34:155–164

Gullone E, King NJ (1991), Acceptability of alternative treatments for school refusal: evaluations by students, caregivers and professionals. *Br J Educ Psychol* 61:346–354

Hampson RB, Hulgus YF, Beavers WR (1991), Comparisons of self-report measures of the Beavers systems model and Olson's circumplex model. *J Fam Psychol* 4:326–340

Hennes HM, Wagner V, Bonadio WA et al. (1990), The effect of oral midazolam on anxiety of preschool children during laceration repair. *Ann Emerg Med* 19:1006–1009

Hersov L (1960), Persistent non-attendance at school. *J Child Psych Psychiatry* 1:130–136

Hersov L (1985), School refusal. In: *Child and Adolescent Psychiatry: Modern Approaches. 2nd* ed, Rutter M, Hersov L, eds. Oxford, England: Blackwell Scientific Publications, pp 382–399

Heyne D, King NJ, Tonge B et al. (1998), The Self-Efficacy Questionnaire for School Situations: development and psychometric evaluation. *Behav Change* 15:31-40

Kearney CA, Albano AM (2000a), *When Children Refuse School: A Cognitive-Behavioral Therapy Approach—Therapist Guide.* San Antonio, TX: Psychological Corporation

Kearney CA, Albano AM (2000b), *When Children Refuse School: A Cognitive-Behavioral Therapy Approach—Parent Workbook.* San Antonio, TX: Psychological Corporation

Kearney CA, Beasley JF (1994), The clinical treatment of school refusal behavior: a survey of referral and practice characteristics. *Psychol Sch* 31:128-132

Kearney CA, Roblek TL (1997), Parent training in the treatment of school refusal behavior. In: *Handbook of Parent Training: Parents as Co-Therapists for Children's Behavior Problems*, 2nd ed, Briesmeister JM, Schaefer CD, eds. New York: Wiley

Kearney CA, Silverman WK (1990), A preliminary analysis of a functional model of assessment and treatment for school refusal behaviour. *Behav Mod* 14:340-366

Kearney CA, Silverman WK (1993), Measuring the function of school refusal behavior: the School Refusal Assessment Scale. *J Clin Child Psychol* 22:85-96

Kearney CA, Silverman WK (1995), Family environment of youngsters with school refusal behavior: a synopsis with implications for assessment and treatment. *Am J Fam Ther* 23:59-72

Kearney [*] CA, Silverman WK (1996), The evolution and reconciliation of taxonomic strategies for school refusal behavior. *Clin Psychol Sci Pract* 3:339-354

Kearney CA, Silverman WK (1999), Functionally based prescriptive and nonprescriptive treatment for children and adolescents with school refusal behavior. *Behav Ther* 30:673-696

Kennedy WA (1965), School phobia: rapid treatment of fifty cases. *J Abnorm Psychol* 70:285-289

King [*] NJ, Ollendick TH, Tonge BJ (1995), *School Refusal: Assessment and Treatment*. Boston: Allyn & Bacon

King NJ, Tonge B, Heyne D, Ollendick TH (2000), Research on the cognitive-behavioral treatment of school refusal: a review and recommendations. *Clin Psychol Rev* 20:495-507

King [*] NJ, Tonge BJ, Heyne D et al. (1998), Cognitive-behavioral treatment of school-refusing children: a controlled evaluation, *J Am Acad Child Adolesc Psychiatry* 37:395-403

Klein RG, Koplewicz HS, Kanner A (1992), Imipramine treatment of children with separation anxiety disorder. *J Am Acad Child Adolesc Psychiatry* 31:21-28

Last [*] CG, Hansen C, Franco N (1998), Cognitive-behavioral treatment of school phobia. *J Am Acad Child Adolesc Psychiatry* 37:404-411

Last CG, Strauss CC (1990), School refusal in anxiety-disordered children and adolescents. *J Am Acad Child Adolesc Psychiatry* 29:31-35

Lee MI, Miltenberger RG (1996), School refusal behavior: classification, assessment and treatment issues. *Educ Treat Child* 19:474-486

March J, Parker J, Sullivan K, Stallings P. Conners CK (1997), The Multidimensional Anxiety Scale for Children (MASC): factor structure, reliabilty, and validity. *J Am Acad Child Adolesc Psychiatry* 36:554-565

Martin C, Cabrol S, Bouvard MP, Lepine JP, Mouren-Simeoni MC (1999), Anxiety and depressive disorders in fathers and mothers of anxious school-refusing children. *J Am Acad Child Adolesc Psychiatry* 38:916-922

Moos RH, Moos BS (1986), *Family Environment Scale Manual*, 2nd ed. Palo Alto, CA: Consulting Psychologists Press

Naylor MW, Staskowski M, Kenney MC, King CA (1994), Language disorders and learning disabilities in school-refusing adolescents. *J Am Acad Child Adolesc Psychiatry* 33:1331-1337

Ollendick TH, King NJ (1998), Assessment practices and issues with school-refusing children. *Behav Change* 15:16-30

Ollendick TH, Mayer JA (1984), School phobia. In: *Behavioral Theories and Treatment of Anxiety*, Turner SM, ed. New York: Plenum, pp 367-411

Olson DH, Bell R, Portner J (1982), *Family Adaptability and Cohesion Evaluation Scale II*. Available from Life Innovations, Family Inventories Project, PO Box 190, Minneapolis, MN 55440-0190

Olson DH, McCubbin HI, Barnes H, Larsen A, Muxen M, Wilson M (1983), *Families: What Makes Them Work.* Beverly Hills, CA: Sage

Pfefferbaum B, Overall JE, Boren HA, Frankel LS, Sullivan MP, Johnson K (1987), Alprazolam in the treatment of anticipatory and acute situational anxiety in children with cancer. *J Am Acad Child Adolesc Psychiatry* 26:532-535

Phelps L, Cox D, Bajorek E (1992), School phobia and separation anxiety: diagnostic and treatment comparisons. *Psychol Sch* 29:384-394

Rapee RM, Barrett PM, Dadds MR, Evans L (1994), Reliability of the DSM-III-R childhood anxiety disorders using structured interview: interrater and parent-child agreement. J *Am Acad Child Adolesc Psychiatry* 33:984-992

Riddle MA, Bernstein GA, Cook EH, Leonard HL, March JS, Swanson JM (1999), Anxiolytics, adrenergic agents, and naltrexone. *J Am Acad Child Adolesc Psychiatry* 38:546-556

Research Units of Pediatric Psychopharmacology Anxiety Study Group (2000), A multi-site double-blind placebo-controlled trial of fluvoxamine for children and adolescents with anxiety disorders. Presented at the 40th New Clinical Drug Evaluation Unit Annual Meeting, Boca Raton, FL, May 30-June 2

Silverman WK, Albano AM (1996), *Anxiety Disorders Interview Schedule for DSM-IV, Child and Parent Versions.* San Antonio, TX: Psychological Corporation

Silverman WK, Rabian B (1995), Test-retest reliabilty of the DSM-III-R childhood anxiety disorder symptoms using the Anxiety Disorders Interview Schedule for Children. *J Anxiety Disord* 9:139-150

Skinner HA, Steinhauer PD, Santa-Barbara J (1983),The Family Assessment Measure. *Can J Commun Ment Health* 2:91-105

Spence SH (1997), The structure of anxiety symptoms among children: a confirmatory factor analytic study. *J Abnorm Psychol* 106:280-297

Steinhauer PD, Santa-Barbara J, Skinner H (1984), The process model of family functioning. *Can J Psychiatry* 29:77-88

Stickney MI, Miltenberger RG (1998), School refusal behavior: prevalence, characteristics, and the schools' response. *Educ Treat Child* 21:160-170

Velosa JF, Riddle MA (2000), Pharmacologic treatment of anxiety disorders in children and adolescents. *Child Adolesc Psychiatr Clin N Am* 9:119-133

Waldron S, Shrier OK, Stone B, Tobin B (1975), School phobia and other childhood neuroses. *Am J Psychiatry* 132:802-808

14

Adolescence: Physical Development

Anorexia Nervosa—Part I

HOW THE MIND STARVES THE BODY, AND WHAT CAN BE DONE TO PREVENT IT

It usually starts with a diet. A teenage girl or young woman begins to eat less and less. She skips meals or takes only tiny portions, often avoiding all but a few kinds of food. She may weigh and measure her food, chew it at length and spit it out, or secretly pocket it and throw it away. Sometimes she uses laxatives and diuretics, or makes herself vomit after meals, and she often exercises compulsively as well. She may say that she looks or feels "fat" although she is obviously becoming emaciated. Her weight sinks and her health deteriorates, but she persists in denying that anything is wrong. She may try to conceal her problem by wearing baggy clothes and avoiding other people.

This demoralizing, debilitating, and sometimes deadly condition is anorexia nervosa. Although the Greek and Latin roots of the words mean "lack of appetite of nervous origin," that description is not quite accurate. Appetite—which is often normal, at least at first—is not even mentioned in the standard psychiatric definition (see below). Researchers are still trying to learn why these women want to starve themselves and how to prevent them from succeeding.

A person with anorexia is likely to be depressed, anxious, irritable, and insomniac. Her joints may become swollen, her hair and skin dry, her nails brittle. She is often lethargic and constipated. She loses bone mass (sometimes permanently), and if she is young enough, her sexual development may be

Harvard Mental Health Letter, Feb 2003, v19, i8, p0.

© 2003 Copyright by President and Fellows of Harvard College.

arrested. Most important, her body temperature, heart rate, and blood pressure can fall to dangerously low levels. Loss of potassium may cause heart arrhythmias. Death from cardiac arrest can occur, as can suicide.

About one in 200 persons in the United States will develop anorexia nervosa at some time. Ninety percent are women. On average, the diagnosis is first made at age 18, but symptoms may arise in much older and much younger people. People with anorexia have a high rate of bulimia, the bingeing and purging syndrome (see *Harvard Mental Health Letter,* July 2002). They are also susceptible to major depression (a rate of 50%–75%) and obsessive-compulsive disorder (a 25% rate).

SYMPTOMS OF ANOREXIA NERVOSA

A person has anorexia nervosa when:

- She (or, occasionally, he) refuses to maintain weight at a normal level. Her weight is 15% below the healthy minimum.
- She shows intense fear of gaining weight or becoming fat.
- She has disturbed ideas about her weight or body shape, tends to judge her value as a person by her weight or body shape, or denies that her weight loss is a serious problem.
- If she is a woman of the appropriate age, she has not menstruated for at least three consecutive cycles.

Anorexia nervosa takes two forms:

- Restricting (dieting, fasting, and compulsive exercise)
- Binge eating/purging (deliberate vomiting or misuse of laxatives, enemas, or diuretics in addition to dieting, fasting, and exercise)

Adapted from the *American Psychiatric Association's Diagnostic and Statistical Manual,* 4th Edition.

THE GENETIC BACKGROUND

Eating disorders run in families. In one recent study, the risk for anorexia in relatives of a person with the disorder turned out to be 11 times higher than average. Studies comparing identical with fraternal twins indicate that the heritability of anorexia (the proportion of individual variability associated with genetic difference) is about 55%.

These statistics have inspired a search for susceptibility genes. Last year, European researchers announced that 11% of anorexics, compared to 4.5% of controls, carried a certain form of the gene for a hormone that stimulates appetite. According to a 2002 report, some people with the restricting type of anorexia nervosa (those who don't binge and purge) have an unusual variant of a gene that affects the reabsorption of the neurotransmitter norepinephrine.

A strain of hogs bred for low fat may provide further data on anorexia susceptibility genes. Some of the hogs are highly active, eat little, and waste away. Researchers are trying to learn whether any similar genetic patterns occur in people suffering from anorexia.

PSYCHOLOGY OF SELF-STARVATION

Physicians have been speculating inconclusively about the psychological roots of anorexia for hundreds of years. Especially in the 20th century, they've suggested a wide range of possible influences, from peer pressure to sexual anxieties and child abuse.

According to one theory, anorexia is a kind of addiction. The German word for the disorder, *Pubert'tsmagersucht,* means "craving for thinness at puberty." One striking characteristic drug addicts and anorexics often have in common is denial—unwillingness to admit that they have a problem. But most experts find more dissimilarities than similarities between anorexia and substance abuse.

There may be something like an anorexic personality, however. Girls and women with the disorder are often shy, neat, quiet, conscientious, and hypersensitive to rejection. They are prey to irrational guilt, feelings of inferiority, and obsessive worrying. They have unrealistic hopes of perfection and feel as though they can never meet their own standards.

Anorexia could be a way some young women with this kind of personality respond to the demands of adulthood. They don't want to be average or admit weakness, but they fear asserting themselves. Their sexual desires and the prospect of independence from their families frighten them. Instead of acknowledging their fears, they try to restore order to their lives by manipulating their weight with compulsive fasting and physical activity.

In that way they exercise some control over their lives. By denying their own physical needs, they show that they won't allow others to dictate them. Falling numbers on the scale are an achievement—a victory over themselves and others. At the same time, by starving themselves and preventing menstruation, they convey the message they don't want to grow up yet.

Some clinicians who treat anorexia believe that, in adolescents at least, the blame lies with parents who make conflicting demands. The theory is that the parents, in effect, tell their daughter to show a capacity for adult independence without separating herself from the family. In the family systems theory of anorexia, it's seen as a defense that maintains the family's otherwise precarious stability. A daughter who refuses to eat may be trying to hold a disintegrating family together by providing a common object of concern for her parents. Or, just the opposite—the family may be "enmeshed," meaning that its boundaries and responsibilities are not distinct. Its members are overprotective of one another; they don't acknowledge feelings or resolve conflicts.

According to this theory, anorexia may arise if the family's rules and roles are too inflexible to change as a daughter grows up.

FASTING AND CULTURE

It's sometimes said that eating disorders in general and anorexia nervosa in particular are largely products of modern Western upper-class and middle-class society. "You can't be too rich or too thin," as the Duchess of Windsor is supposed to have said. In industrial countries, the average woman is becoming heavier, while the body regarded as ideal for health and beauty becomes slimmer. Being happy and successful, women are told, goes with being thin. As a result, more than half of American women, including many young girls, say they are on a diet.

Of course, the vast majority of people who diet don't have an eating disorder. But the more intense this kind of social pressure is, the more likely it seems that a troubled young woman will develop anorexia rather than (or in addition to) other psychiatric symptoms. And now, the argument goes, anorexia, along with bulimia and obesity, is beginning to infect the non-Western world, carried by television, films, and advertisements.

But research has shown that it's not so simple. Symptoms that would now be called anorexia nervosa were reported as early as the 17th century in England. Descriptions of similar symptoms also appear in ancient Chinese and Persian manuscripts and in African tribal lore. Today, many studies show no clear relationship between severe eating disorders and social class or the influence of Western culture.

There is some (disputed) evidence that women in non-Western countries are, on the average, less dissatisfied with their bodies, but that doesn't necessarily imply a lower probability of anorexia. In the United States, whites report more mild eating disturbances than African Americans, but the two groups have about the same rate of clinical eating disorders, including anorexia. Although middle-class anorexia patients may get more attention, it has not been shown that anorexia is a function of social class, either.

Women with anorexia may not even be especially prone to over-estimating the size of their bodies. One study comparing anorexic with healthy women of the same height and weight found that both groups overestimated their size by about the same amount. The anorexic women were more anxious about their body shape only because they had unreasonable standards.

In some parts of the world, symptoms resembling anorexia occur without any apparent fear of being fat. Anorexic women in Hong Kong may say that they have family problems, their appetite is poor, or they simply don't know why they can't eat. In Ghana, women with anorexic symptoms often say they are fasting for religious reasons.

In medieval Europe, for some centuries, fasting almost unto death was regarded as a sign of holiness—a withdrawal from the world and the flesh.

One famous medieval ascetic was St. Catherine of Siena, who died at age 32 in 1379, apparently from the effects of starvation. She wrote, "Make a supreme effort to root out that self-love from your heart and to plant in its place this holy self-hatred. This is the royal road by which we turn our back on mediocrity and which leads us without fail to the summit of perfection."

Today's anorexic girls and young women often confess similar thoughts of self-denial and self-perfection. The American Psychiatric Association now classifies a condition with all the symptoms of anorexia nervosa except an obsession with body shape or size as an example of an "eating disorder not otherwise specified."

It's possible that cultures supply only the justification for self-starvation rather than its cause. Some feminists have proposed that women who refuse to eat are misguided rebels making an inarticulate social protest. By refusing to develop a woman's body, they are rejecting a woman's place, whatever that may be in a given culture. Their refusal to eat is a way to show that they are exceptional. How they describe what they are doing—dieting to become thin or fasting to become holy, for example—may depend on the social pressures and opportunities they face.

RESOURCES

National Association of Anorexia Nervosa and Associated Disorders
P.O. Box 7
Highland Park, IL 60035
(847) 831-3438
www.anad.org

Anorexia Nervosa and Related Eating Disorders (ANRED) Inc.,
P.O. Box 5102
Eugene, OR 97405
(503) 344-1144
www.anred.com

National Eating Disorders Association
603 Stewart St., Suite 803
Seattle, WA 98101
(206) 382-3587
www.nationaleatingdisorders.org

THE CAUSAL CONUNDRUM

All the biological, psychological, and cultural explanations of anorexia are speculative, because cause and effect are so difficult to discern among the tangled roots of the disorder. For example, starvation itself causes psychological symptoms. In a classic study, young conscientious objectors to the military draft volunteered to undergo near-starvation. Within six months, as their weight fell to 75% of its original level, they developed many psychological symptoms typical of anorexia. Even their responses to a personality questionnaire changed.

Or consider the influence of families. The parents of a girl who refuses to eat are under great strain, and the family is bound to be in turmoil. And a young woman with an eating disorder is likely to be dissatisfied with her mother and father because they are dissatisfied with her. She may regard them as intrusive and abusive if they criticize and try to change her, or as indifferent and neglectful if they try to avoid conflict.

Take a woman who is predisposed (perhaps genetically) to depression, anxiety, and self-defeating perfectionism, or one who has serious family troubles. Suppose she has been persuaded that everyone admires women who are relentlessly self-disciplined, whether that means being slender, athletic, or ascetic. She diets (or fasts), and the resulting changes in her body and brain make normal eating still more difficult. Her anxiety and depression become worse, along with her physical health.

But that is only one way it could happen. In the end, explanations of anorexia are unique stories best pieced together by the individual patient with the help of a professional. When the story is told, patients and therapists can work together to find a solution.

(To be continued)

CRITICAL THINKING QUESTIONS

1. What evidence is presented in this article that supports that idea that anorexia is genetically or biologically determined? What evidence is presented that supports cultural causes?
2. There is evidence that family dynamics may either cause or sustain anorexia. Explain how this evidence may not be a causal relationship but may be one more of a correlational relationship.

REFERENCES

American Psychiatric Association. *Practice Guideline for the Treatment of Patients with Eating Disorders,* Second Edition. American Psychiatric Press, 2000.

Fairburn CG and Brownell KD, eds. *Eating Disorders and Obesity: A Comprehensive Handbook.* Second Edition, Guilford Press, 2002.

Herrin M and Matsumoto N. *The Parent's Guide to Childhood Eating Disorders.* Owl Books, 2002.

Polivy J and Herman CP. "Causes of Eating Disorders," *Annual Review of Psychology* (2002): Vol. 53, pp. 187–213.

Sargent JT. *The Long Road Back: A Survivor's Guide to Anorexia.* North Star Publications, 1999.

Vitiello B and Lederhendler I. "Research on Eating Disorders: Current Status and Future Prospects," *Biological Psychiatry* (2000): Vol. 47, No. 9, pp. 777–86.

Anorexia Nervosa—Part II

In part I we discussed the symptoms of anorexia nervosa and its possible roots in heredity, upbringing, and culture. In part II we describe treatments, the evidence for their effectiveness, and long-term outcomes.

A severely anorexic patient may need help from several kinds of therapy and the services of psychiatrists, physicians, nurses, and dietitians. The aim is to restore her weight, change her eating (and thinking) habits, and treat associated psychiatric disorders, while enlisting the support of family members and providing help for them if necessary.

Doctors recommend hospitalization of a person with anorexia when she won't otherwise agree to treatment although her weight has been more than 20% below the healthy range for several months, or when she is developing life-threatening physical symptoms or is in danger of committing suicide. Day care is an alternative for patients with less severe symptoms and at various stages of recovery.

Regaining weight is a priority, and the usual method is a simple form of behavior therapy. Patients eat frequent small meals under a nurse's supervision and are forbidden to leave anything on the tray. They are praised for eating and gaining weight and may be rewarded with greater freedom of movement or more visiting privileges. After leaving the hospital, they often follow a plan set by a dietitian, who may ask them to record what they eat and when.

PSYCHOTHERAPY

Studies have shown that anorexic patients who leave the hospital before their weight returns to normal are more likely to relapse. But regaining weight is no guarantee of recovery, any more than detoxification (supervised withdrawal) is a guarantee of recovery for a heroin addict or alcoholic. The minds of anorexic patients, as well as their bodies, must change. The trouble is that what they fear most—normal eating and normal weight—is what they need most. It's a challenge to convince them that they'll be better off without a habit that has given their lives meaning.

Therapists often use cognitive techniques to correct the false beliefs anorexic patients have, about food and about themselves. The therapist and patient explore her tendency to think in extremes, her food and exercise rituals, her harsh self-criticism and perfectionism, and her self-centered interpretations of other people's behavior. The therapist may try to refute vague fears, make implicit thoughts explicit, help the patient look at herself from a different point of view (she feels fat but says that others of the same height and

Harvard Mental Health Letter, March 2003, v19, i9, p0.

© 2003 Copyright by President and Fellows of Harvard College. All Rights Reserved.

weight are too thin), and help her achieve a better sense of body size and the amount of food she's eating.

Motivational enhancement techniques that strengthen the desire for recovery may also help some patients. While they are gaining weight, supportive psychotherapy that provides sympathy, coaching, and encouragement may be useful. When the patient's weight is nearly normal, some therapists move on to a more insight-oriented treatment, examining experiences that may have led to the condition.

Some experts doubt the usefulness of support groups for anorexic patients, especially when they lack professional supervision. The problem is that these groups may reinforce denial. Group members may begin to regard themselves as an exclusive club of elite hunger artists. If that happens, at best they'll be seeking mutual approval and acceptance rather than change. At worst, they may compete to see who can eat the least or tell the most fascinating stories, while exchanging advice on how to fake weight gain or conceal food.

ADVICE FOR PARENTS OF A CHILD WITH ANOREXIA

- Don't scold, criticize, or nag.
- Try to be with her at meals even if she won't eat, but don't change your eating or food buying habits to accommodate her.
- Don't discuss food while eating with her.
- Don't discuss your own weight or eating habits.
- Don't discuss her looks—or your own or anyone else's.
- Always emphasize health rather than appearance or weight.
- Encourage her to get professional help.
- Consider family or couple's therapy.
- Make it clear that you understand her feelings of being worthless and undeserving. But direct comments may sound like accusations. It's better to talk about your own feelings:
- "I'm afraid you are hurting yourself."
- "I know that when people tell you that you look healthier, you think they mean you look fat, but I mean you seem more relaxed and your eyes are brighter."
- "It's affecting my life so much that I've consulted a doctor myself."

People who have recovered from anorexia often say it was important that friends and relatives kept trying to reach them, even if that meant repeatedly delivering the same message and apparently getting no response.

Source: Anorexia Nervosa and Related Eating Disorders, Inc.

MEDICATIONS

Medications play a minor role in the treatment of anorexia. Anorexic patients are predictably reluctant to take drugs, and the side effects can be uncomfortable for them or even dangerous to their enfeebled bodies. After they gain some weight, antidepressants may reduce the risk of relapse and rehospitalization, especially for people with severe depression or obsessive-compulsive symptoms. Because of their relatively mild side effects, selective serotonin reuptake inhibitors (SSRIs) are usually the best choice. Occasionally an antianxiety drug or a novel antipsychotic medication may be useful. Electroconvulsive therapy and estrogens have no proven value.

TREATMENT: THE EVIDENCE

There's little evidence on the effectiveness of psychotherapy for anorexia, and most of it comes from case reports and clinical experience. Of the few controlled studies, most have measured success only by weight gain, and they have followed patients for only a few months, although anorexia nervosa is usually a chronic illness.

In one meta-analysis, behavior therapy was superior to medications in shortening hospital stays and restoring weight. Programs using only bed rest for failure to eat were as effective as stricter regimens with fixed eating requirements or scheduled weight gain linked to privileges like permission to exercise or receive visitors. A 2002 review of 20 controlled trials of psychotherapy found that it was questionably effective, except for family therapy with younger women who had been ill for a relatively short time.

IN THE LONG RUN

Recovery may take a long time, with many relapses, and it is often incomplete. Even when the most serious symptoms go away, patients often have various residual effects and chronic troubles. They also have a high death rate—one of the highest among psychiatric disorders, as much as 10%–20% in 20 years. Although anorexia is often considered a disorder of the young, it is most deadly in older women (and men), because older bodies are less resilient and the eating habits of adults can't easily be supervised.

Some typical findings come from a recent review of studies in which hospitalized patients with anorexia were followed for four years or more. The outcome was good (nearly normal weight and regular menstruation) for 44%, poor for 24%, and moderate for 28%. Two-thirds were still preoccupied with food and weight, many were more or less depressed, and up to 40% had symptoms of bulimia. One in 20 (5%) had died.

FOR THE FUTURE

Our understanding of anorexia is limited, and there is plenty of room for discovery. The search for genes related to the disorder continues. Brain scans may show the responses associated with patients' hunger and body image before and during recovery from anorexia. Psychological and cultural influences will become less mysterious with more study of anorexia symptoms at different stages of life and in different societies. When we know more, even the definition of the disorder may change to include refusal to eat that is not related to concerns about body shape or weight. Researchers will also learn from the study of psychiatric disorders that accompany anorexia and its impact on families.

HORMONES AND ANOREXIA

Study of the hormonal systems that regulate food intake and energy output may some day contribute to the prevention and cure of anorexia nervosa. The thyroid and adrenal glands, under the direction of the brain, control the circulation of hormones, including cortisol and adrenaline, which influence eating habits along with mood and responses to stress.

Scientists recently discovered hormones devoted specifically to appetite regulation. Leptin, discovered in 1994, is made by fat cells and activates brain pathways that cause appetite loss. Its function is to let the body know that it has no need for food because sufficient energy is stored in the form of fat. When leptin levels fall, metabolism slows and appetite increases. Ghrelin (pronounced gray-lin), discovered only two years ago, is secreted in the stomach and intestines and serves as an appetite stimulant. Ghrelin levels rise in people who lose weight. Several other intestinal hormones, including cholecystokinin (CCK), are also involved in appetite regulation.

It is a complicated system that can go wrong in several ways. Animals bred for inability to synthesize leptin overeat and become grotesquely obese. Bodies and brains can also develop resistance to appetite-regulating hormones. Obese people have high levels of leptin, but apparently do not respond to it. Anorexic patients have high levels of ghrelin, which fall when they begin to gain weight.

A drug that increased the response to ghrelin or reduced the response to leptin might help treat wasting diseases, such as AIDS and some cancers. Whether it would help people with anorexia nervosa is less clear because loss of appetite is not a cause of that disorder or even one of its defining symptoms. When stressed by deliberate self-starvation, the body may stop responding normally to hormones, but anorexia originates elsewhere. It is a condition in which eating is not reinforced because resisting the body's hunger quiets the mind's anxieties and so fulfills its desires. The solution to anorexia nervosa may lie in the circuitry that connects appetite-regulating and stress hormone systems with the brain's reward and fear centers.

Discovering more about the causes of anorexia should help in the development of treatments. Many combinations of group, individual, and family therapies have never been tested. Medications, now of little use, may become more important as scientists learn more about appetite-regulating hormones. Finally, there is the ultimate goal of prevention, possibly attainable some day by screening young women for early signs of the disorder.

RESOURCES

American Anorexia/Bulimia Association, Inc.
165 West 46th Street, Suite 1108
New York, NY 10036
(212) 575-6200
www.4women.gov/nwhic/references/mdreferrals/aaba.htm

Anorexia Nervosa and Related Eating Disorders, Inc. (ANRED)
Post Office Box 5102
Eugene, OR 97405
(503) 344-1144
www.anred.com

National Association of Anorexia Nervosa and Associated Disorders
Post Office Box 7
Highland Park, IL 60035
(847) 831-3438
www.anad.org

National Eating Disorders Association
603 Stewart Street, Suite 803
Seattle, WA 98101
(206) 382-3587
www.nationaleatingdisorders.org

CRITICAL THINKING QUESTIONS

1. Summarize the mainstream forms of treatment and rate each in terms of effectiveness based on research data. If you were choosing a form of treatment for your son or daughter, which would you choose? Explain why.
2. What do you surmise about the prognosis of children with anorexia? Is it a disorder for which there is a complete recovery?
3. Look over the list of suggestions for parents. Are there any others that you think should be added or deleted? Explain your answers.

REFERENCES

American Psychiatric Association. *Practice Guideline for the Treatment of Patients with Eating Disorders,* Second Edition. American Psychiatric Press, 2000.

Fairburn CG and Brownell KD, eds. *Eating Disorders and Obesity: A Comprehensive Handbook.* Second Edition, Guilford Press, 2002.

Herrin M and Matsumoto N. *The Parent's Guide to Childhood Eating Disorders.* Owl Books, 2002.

Lock J, et al. *Treatment Manual for Anorexia Nervosa: A Family-Based Approach.* Guilford Press, 2000.

Polivy J and Herman CP. "Causes of Eating Disorders," *Annual Review of Psychology* (2002): Vol. 53, pp. 187–213.

Sargent JT. *The Long Road Back: A Survivor's Guide to Anorexia.* North Star Publications, 1999.

Vitiello B and Lederhendler I. "Research on Eating Disorders: Current Status and Future Prospects," *Biological Psychiatry* (2000): Vol. 47, No. 9, pp. 777–86.

Wildes JE, et al. "The Roles of Ethnicity and Culture in the Development of Eating Disturbance and Body Dissatisfaction: A Meta-Analytic Review," *Clinical Psychology Review* (2001): Vol. 21, No. 4, pp. 521–51.

15

Adolescence: Cognitive Development

Adolescent Risk Taking and Self-Reported Injuries Associated with Substance Use

Anthony Spirito, Elissa Jelalian, Deborah Rasile,
Cynthia Rohrbeck, and Lyn Vinnick

Objective: To examine the incidence of adolescent substance use at the time of injury and its relation to risk-taking behavior. Method: A total of 643 male and 782 female 9th through 12th grade students at three high schools anonymously completed surveys on any injuries that had occurred in the prior 6 months associated with substance use and risk-taking behavior. Results: Males reported a higher incidence of injuries related to alcohol or other drugs than females (17.3% vs. 13%). The 17 year olds reported more injuries related to substance use than 14 or 15 year olds (20.2% vs. 14.4% and 15%, respectively). A logistic regression analysis revealed that the odds of a substance use-related injury increased approximately sixfold when adolescents reported engaging in risk-taking behavior. Conclusion: A significant portion of adolescents (approximately 15%) reported injuries associated with substance use. Adolescents who reported a history of risk-taking behaviors were much more likely to report substance use-related injuries.

American Journal of Drug and Alcohol Abuse, Feb 2000, v26, i1, p113.

© 2000 Marcel Dekker, Inc.

INTRODUCTION

Adolescence has often been characterized as a time of increased experimentation and exploration with a range of risky behaviors, including substance use. Substance use has also been implicated in adolescent trauma and has been found to result in more frequent occurrences of injury and more serious injury (1). Much of the research that has been conducted on alcohol use and injury during adolescence has focused on drinking and driving behaviors (2). Often overlooked is the role of alcohol and other drugs in other types of injuries.

A recent review article suggests that there is a consistent heightened risk for injury with alcohol consumption across many adult injuries (3). There is some empirical evidence documenting the importance of alcohol in adolescents who experience traumatic and fatal injuries, including drowning and falls (1, 4). Several studies have examined the presence of alcohol in adolescents who present to emergency departments (EDs) with trauma. Hicks et al. (5) retrospectively examined 878 records of injured adolescents (16 to 20 years old) presenting to an ED over a 4-year period. A blood alcohol concentration (BAC) was ordered on 53% of the cases, and in 68% of these cases, the BAC was positive. Another study (6) found that, in a population of 134 patients between 13 and 19 years of age seen for trauma-related injuries, 34% of those screened had test results that were positive for alcohol or drugs of abuse. They also reported a significantly higher percentage of positive toxicology screens among adolescents admitted with intentional injuries (gunshot wounds, stab wounds, assaults) as compared to those with unintentional injuries (falls and vehicular trauma). Adolescents presenting to a trauma center who had positive serum alcohol concentrations had a greater probability of having a psychiatric history and more often had a prior or subsequent injury (7).

Although there is some evidence documenting the role of alcohol use in adolescent traumatic injury, few studies have examined the relationship between alcohol and other drugs and nontraumatic injury (such as cuts or from falling or an athletic activity). Furthermore, minimal attention has been paid to other behavioral factors that may contribute to these types of injuries. One construct that has been related to substance use during adolescence is risk-taking behavior (8, 9). Risk-taking behavior has been commonly defined as behavior that is volitional and has a potentially noninjurious outcome, as well as an outcome that may result in harm (10). Risk-taking behavior is considered by many to be a normal part of adolescence. However, many risky behaviors, such as unsafe sex and failure to use seatbelts in motor vehicles, can result in injury, harm, or even death and may be influenced by alcohol and other drug use. In one of the few surveillance studies exploring alcohol use and risky behaviors, alcohol use and physically risky behavior tended to occur together in 8th and 10th graders (11).

The present study was designed to survey the incidence of injuries associated with alcohol and other drugs and to examine the relationship between risk-taking behavior and substance use-related nontraumatic injury in a sample of high school students. Consistent with previous research (12, 13), it was expected that males would have higher rates of injuries associated with alcohol and other drugs than females, and that older adolescents would have higher rates than younger adolescents. It was also hypothesized that there would be a significant relationship between risk-taking behavior and injuries associated with alcohol and other drugs.

METHOD

Subjects

A total of 1688 students in the 9th through 12th grades from three high schools in the Northeast were surveyed. The three high schools were selected to provide a demographically diverse sample, particularly in regard to socioeconomic status. The metropolitan area from which these subjects were drawn contained about 1 million persons. No one directly refused to complete the survey; however, 205 subjects returned surveys with missing data; these surveys were eliminated. Any subject reporting a logical inconsistency on an item (e.g., if a subject reported medical treatment, but no injury) was eliminated from the survey ($N = 58$), resulting in an 84% response rate and a total sample of 1425 (643 males, 782 females). Most of the eliminated cases had completed information on age and gender. These eliminated cases were slightly older than the final sample, 16.3 [+ or −] 1.1 years versus 16.0 [+ or −] 1.2 years, $t(1638) = 3.45$, $p < .01$. There were no gender differences, χ^2 $(1, N = 1634) = 1.10$, n.s.

One high school was a "magnet" school (i.e., admission is based on ranking from an entrance exam) in an urban area. There were 248 males and 410 females (mean age = 16.2 years, SD = 1.0 years). The median family income for the city was $14,948. The second school was a regional suburban high school where the median income for the community was $18,000. There were 129 males and 99 females (mean age = 16.0 years, SD = 1.1 years). The third school was also a suburban neighborhood. The median income of this community was $27,900. There were 266 males and 273 females (mean age = 16.4 years, SD = 1.2 years).

Procedure

High school students were administered, in their classrooms, self-report questionnaires on risk taking, perception of injury risk, and injuries (see below). Only results on substance use-related injuries and risk taking are reported here. This protocol was approved by school district superintendents, school principals, and the hospital institutional review board. All instructions were read aloud by one of the investigators or a teacher. No identifying information was collected beyond age, gender, and grade. The instructions read as follows:

> Thank you for agreeing to participate in today's survey. Your participation here is completely voluntary. If you don't feel comfortable with a

question, you don't have to answer it. You will not be identified personally in any way. Please do not put your name on this page or any of the following pages.

On the following pages, you will be asked a number of questions dealing with your thoughts and opinions on different things teenagers do. You also will be asked questions about accidents, injuries, or other ways you got hurt in the last 6 months. Please be sure to read the instructions carefully. Please try to answer the questions honestly. There are no right or wrong answers; it is your opinions that are important. All of your responses will be kept in the strictest of confidence. If you should have any questions while taking the survey, please feel free to ask the interviewer about it. The interviewer is here to help you understand the instructions and procedures.

Measures

Adolescent Injury Checklist (AIC). The AIC is a self-report measure developed for this study that records injuries that occurred in the prior 6 months. The AIC has 17 items, covering both major injuries (e.g., secondary to car crashes, gunshot wounds) and minor injuries (e.g., cuts, falls). The AIC was adapted from an early version of the Child Health and Illness Profile—Adolescent Edition (14), a survey developed to assess positive and negative health behaviors in adolescence comprehensively. In this adaptation, if an injury is reported, adolescents also answer whether alcohol or other drugs were used about the time of the injury. Each item endorsed receives a score of 1, and a total score for substance use-related injuries is calculated by summing all individual substance use-related injury items except the "Other" item. Internal consistency in this sample, as measured by an alpha coefficient, was .67 for the items on substance use-related injury occurrence.

Risk-Taking Scale (RTS). The RTS is a four-item scale that was developed for large school-based survey studies (15). The items on the RTS include engaging in risky sports, doing risky things for fun, taking chances when out at night, and engaging in dangerous behaviors for the thrill of it. The items were subjected to a principal components analysis with a varimax rotation. One factor with an eigenvalue greater than 1 emerged. This factor was composed of all four items with factor loadings ranging from .38 to .73, had an eigenvalue of 2.39, and accounted for 59.7% of the variance. Scores on the scale ranged from 0 to 4. Internal consistency for the new scale was calculated at 0.77.

RESULTS

Preliminary Analyses

The frequency of injuries associated with alcohol or other drugs by gender, age, and race is presented in Table 1. For females, their mean age was 16.2 yrs (SD = 1.1 years); their mean score on the AIC was 0.2 (SD = 0.8), and it was 1.6 (SD = 1.8) on the RTS. For males, their mean age was 16.3 years (SD = 1.1 years); their mean score on the AIC was 0.4 (SD = 1.0), and it was 2.8 (SD = 2.4) on the RTS. Because of the relatively small number of 18 year olds, we first compared 17 and 18 year olds on their AIC and RTS scores to determine if the two age groups could be combined. There was no difference on either the AIC [t(417) = 1.13, n.s.] or RTS [t(417) = 1.21, n.s.] scores by age. Consequently, 17 and 18 year olds were combined into one group.

Table 1. Percentage of Alcohol-Related Injuries Broken by Gender, Age, and Race as Reported by High School Students

	%	N	%	N
GENDER				
Male	82.7	532	8.4	54
Female	87.0	680	7.3	57
AGE IN YEARS				
14	92.5	196	2.8	6
15	85.6	332	9.3	36
16	85.0	345	7.1	29
17	79.8	368	9.8	33
18	85.5	71	8.4	7
RACE				
Caucasian	83.6	817	8.6	84
Hispanic	95.0	96	2.0	2
African-American	87.1	54	8.1	5
Asian	93.1	95	2.0	2
GENDER				
Male	3.3	21	2.2	14
Female	3.5	27	1.4	11
AGE IN YEARS				
14	2.8	6	0.5	1
15	2.1	8	2.6	10
16	3.7	15	2.0	8
17	4.8	16	1.5	5
18	3.6	3	1.2	1
RACE				
Caucasian	4.2	41	1.7	17
Hispanic	0.0	0	2.0	2

Table 1. (*Continued*)

	%	N	%	N
RACE				
African-American	1.6	1	0.0	0
Asian	2.0	2	1.0	1
GENDER				
Male	3.4	22		
Female	0.9	7		
AGE IN YEARS				
14	1.4	3		
15	0.5	2		
16	2.2	9		
17	4.2	14		
18	1.2	1		
RACE				
Caucasian	1.8	18		
Hispanic	1.0	1		
African-American	3.2	2		
Asian	2.0	2		

Note: May not total 100% due to rounding.

A significant difference by gender was found on the AIC [$t(1424) = 2.35$, $p < .05$.] Males reported significantly higher substance use-related injuries than females. A significant difference by gender was also reported on the RTS [$t(1423) = 11.11$, $p < .0001$], with males reporting significantly more risk-taking behaviors than females.

Significant differences by age in the rate of substance use-related injuries were also found on the AIC [$F(4,1421) = 3.87$, $p < .01$]. Post hoc testing with a Tukey procedure revealed that 17/18 year olds reported more injuries associated with alcohol or other drugs than 14 or 15 year olds. The interaction of age and gender on injuries associated with alcohol or other drugs of the AIC was not significant, $F(4,1424) = 2.35$, $p = .06$. Significant age differences were not found on the RTS, $F(4,1420) = 1.35$, n.s.

To ensure a sufficiently large sample size for each group, analyses by racial groups were limited to the four major subgroups: white, African-American, Hispanic, and Southeast Asian. A significant difference by race was not found on substance use-related injuries by the AIC [$F(3,1241) = 2.02$, n.s.] or the RTS [$F(3,1238) = 2.40$, $p = .07$].

There was a significant difference on number of substance use-related injuries by school, $F(2,1424) = 8.57$, $p < .001$. Post hoc analyses revealed that the suburban school subjects reported more substance use-related injuries than those in the magnet school. There was also a significant difference on the RTS by school, $F(2,1422) = 4.18$, $p < .05$. Post hoc testing with a Tukey test revealed that the regional suburban school had higher risk-taking scores than the magnet school. Of the 1425 subjects with valid data, 213 adolescents reported substance use-related injuries: 7.8% reported one substance use-related injury in the prior 6 months, 3.4% reported two, 1.8% reported three, and 2% reported four or more.

The percentage of substance use-related injuries was also examined separately for each injury. The most common injuries reported to be associated with alcohol or other drugs were cuts, burns, and physical fights, occurring in 4.8%, 2.9%, and 2.1% of the sample, respectively. When each of the substance use-related injuries was examined by gender using χ^2 analyses, no significant differences were found.

Bivariate Analyses

For males, the Pearson product-moment correlation between substance use-related injuries and risk taking was .37 ($p < .0001$). The Kendall tau between substance use-related injuries and age was. 11 (n.s.), and it was .01 (n.s.) between race and substance use-related injuries. For females, the Pearson correlation between substance use-related injuries and risk taking was .39 ($p < .0001$); the Kendall tau between substance use-related injuries and age was .04 (n.s.), and it was. 11 (n.s.) between race and substance use-related injuries. Fisher Z statistics were calculated to determine if differences in the magnitude of the correlation coefficients by gender were statistically significant. Neither of the differences between males and females for the correlations between substance use-related injuries and risk taking ($Z = 0.44$, n.s.) or substance use-related injuries and age ($Z = 1.46$, n.s.) were statistically significant.

To understand better the differences between those with and without injuries associated with alcohol or other drugs, the sample was subdivided into those not reporting such an injury ($N = 1212$) and those reporting one or more substance use-related injuries ($N = 213$). The group reporting substance use-related injuries reported higher scores on risk taking ($N = 21.2$, $SD = 5.1$) than the group not reporting substance use-related injuries ($M = 16.0$, $SD = 4.4$), $t(1423) = 15.56$, $p < .0001$.

Regression Analyses

Two logistic regression analyses, one for males (Table 2) and one for females (Table 3), were conducted to determine which variables best predicted substance use-related injuries (coded yes or no). School was entered into the regression equation on the first step as a covariate because it represented location and median income differences that were not directly interpretable or the major focus of interest in this study. Age and ethnicity were entered on the second step, and risktaking, the variable of most interest, on the third step.

Table 2. Results of Logistic Regression Predicting Injuries Associated with Alcohol or Other Drugs Among Males (N = 643)

			Odds	χ^2
Step	Variables	Beta	Ratio	Improvement
1	School	−.40	1.50	19.23
2	Demographics		11.14	
	Race	.45	1.57	
	Age	.29	1.34	
3	Risk taking	.30	1.35	43.35
		χ^2		
Step	Variables	df	model	df
1	School	1	19.23(a)	1
2	Demographics	1	30.37(b)	3
	Race			
	Age			
3	Risk taking	1	73.72(a)	4

Note: Because race, age, and risk taking are on scales with different units of measurement, these odds ratios need to be adjusted to be interpreted (see Results).
(a) $p < .0001$.
(b) $p < .01$.

Table 3. Results of Logistic Regression Predicting Injuries Associated with Alcohol or Other Drugs Among Females (N = 782)

			Odds	χ^2
Step	Variables	Beta	Ratio	Improvement
1	School	−.34	1.41	16.40
2	Demographics		5.00	
	Race	−.35	1.40	
	Age	.20	1.23	
3	Risk taking	.46	1.59	72.18
		χ^2		
Step	Variables	df	model	df
1	School	1	16.40(a)	1
2	Demographics	1	21.40	3
	Race			
	Age			
3	Risk taking	1	93.58(a)	4

Note: Because race, age, and risk taking are on scales with different units of measurement, these odds ratios need to be adjusted to be interpreted (see Discussion).
(a) $p < .0001$.

Because age had a curvilinear relationship with substance use-related injuries, age was categorized into 14 years olds, 15 year olds, 16 year olds, and 17-18 year olds. Results are shown in Tables 2 and 3. For males, school, age, and risk taking were significant predictors in the final model, while only school and risk taking were predictors for females. The odds of being involved in a substance use-related injury increased for males and females by the school attended and their reported involvement in risk-taking behaviors. Older males were also more likely to incur a substance use-related injury than younger teenage males.

DISCUSSION

This survey indicated that approximately 15% of adolescents report an injury associated with alcohol or other drugs in the prior 6 months. Most of the injuries were minor. This rate is lower than that found in studies conducted in EDs (e.g., 34%) [6], but still is substantial. As hypothesized, males had a statistically higher rate of substance use-related injury than females. However, the rates were comparable (17.3% vs. 13%). The hypothesis that older adolescents would report more substance use-related injuries was partially confirmed. The rates of such injuries appear to peak at 17 and 18 years of age. Since this study was conducted in schools, the rates of substance use-related injuries for older adolescents in the general population may be higher because school dropouts are included. No racial differences were noted on the incidence of injuries associated with alcohol or other drugs. The finding of higher rates of substance use-related injury in the suburban school than in the magnet school is somewhat difficult to interpret. One possibility is that school serves as a proxy variable for socioeconomic status. An alternative interpretation is that students attending the magnet school represent a sample that is more academically oriented and less inclined to engage in substance use.

The hypothesis that there would be a positive relationship between self-reported risk-taking behavior and substance use-related injury in adolescents was supported. When risk taking was reported, the odds of an injury associated with substance use increased significantly. Risk taking increased the odds of a substance use-related injury by 1.35 in males and 1.59 in females. Rather than the standard interpretation of an odds ratio with dichotomous predictors, it should be kept in mind that when continuous predictors, such as risk taking in this study, are used, the odds ratio refers to change in odds for each unit change in the predictor. Thus, because risk taking was entered into the regression equation as a linear variable, a more accurate way to interpret this finding is to ask what the odds are of incurring a substance use-related injury if a subject scores one standard deviation above the mean on risk taking. Because the standard deviation is approximately 5, the odds will increase 1.35 for males with each unit increase of risk taking. Thus, the total odds increase is more than sixfold (5×1.35).

This relationship between risk taking and substance use-related injury held across a diverse sample and did not differ by gender. Few studies have examined the relationship between risk taking and injury, and even fewer have examined injuries associated with alcohol or other drugs. Consequently, it is difficult to compare these findings to the literature. One study (16) did not find that high levels of sensation seeking were related to sports-related injuries. Another study (11) with a similar methodology found a relationship between alcohol use and physically risky behavior in adolescents, regardless of age or gender.

Several cautions are in order with regard to interpretation of these findings. The substance use-related and medically treated injuries were not verified. Further investigation of the psychometrics of the AIC is also needed. Rates of adolescent injury have been shown to be significantly higher when self-report data are based on 1-month rather than 1-year recall (17). Consequently, self-report based on a 6-month recall in this study may underestimate injury. In addition, because assessment of both risk taking and substance use-related injury occurred at a single point in time, the same recall bias may have affected reports of risk taking, substance use, and injury.

The results of this study suggest that prevention of adolescent injury may be enhanced if attention is paid not only to the role of alcohol and other drugs, but also to risk-taking behavior and the potentiating role of alcohol and other drugs in increasing risk-taking behavior, which in turn may increase risk of injury. Studies with adults suggest that alcohol use impairs a young adult's ability to perceive negative consequences, which increases risk-taking behavior while intoxicated (18). These risk-taking behaviors might then increase the risk of injury. Alternatively, adolescent risk takers may be more likely to use alcohol and other drugs, which then places them at risk for injury. Future research in this area should include more detailed assessment of these behaviors (i.e., risk-taking and substance use associated with injuries) as well as the sequencing of these behaviors in youth. These types of studies may provide additional important information that can be used in prevention efforts.

ACKNOWLEDGMENT

Thanks to Chantelle Nobile and Melissa McGuinn for assisting in the analysis of these data.

CRITICAL THINKING QUESTIONS

1. What were the original hypotheses proposed by the researchers regarding risk-taking behavior and injuries? In what ways were these hypotheses supported or not supported by the data?

2. Compare and contrast risk-taking behaviors and injuries in males and females, age, race, and school. What conclusions can be drawn from this information?
3. How do you think this information could be used to impact risk-taking behavior in adolescents? In what ways could it be useful for adolescents, parents, teachers, or health care providers?

REFERENCES

1. Bass, J., Gallagher, S., and Mehta, K., Injuries to adolescents and young adults, *Pedi Clin. No Amer* 32:31–39 (1985).
2. Blose, J., and Holder, H., Utilization in a problem drinking population, *Am. J. Public Health* 81:1571–1575 (1991).
3. Cherpitel, C., J., Alcohol and injuries: a review of international emergency room studies, *Addiction* 88:651–665 (1993).
4. Friedman, I., Alcohol and unnatural deaths in San Francisco youth, *Pediatrics* 76:191–193 (1985).
5. Hicks, B., Morris, J., Bass, S., et al., Alcohol and the adolescent trauma population, *J. Pediatr. Surg.* 25:944–949 (1990).
6. Loiselle, J., Baker, M., Templeton, J., et al., Substance abuse in adolescent trauma, *Ann. Emerg. Med.* 22:24–28 (1993).
7. Maio, R., Portnoy, J., Blow, F., et al., Injury type, injury severity, and repeat occurrence of substance use-related trauma in adolescents, *Alcohol. Clin. Exp. Res.* 18:261–264 (1994).
8. Donovan, J., and Jessor, R., Structure of problem behavior in adolescence and young adulthood, *J. Consult. Clin. Psychol.* 53:890–904 (1985).
9. Jessor, R., Donovan, J. E., and Costa, F. M., Problem drinking and risky driving among youth: a psychosocial approach to a lifestyle pattern, Proc. Int. Workshop: High Alcohol Consumers and Traffic (ACTes INRETS) 18:137–152 (1989).
10. Irwin, C. E., Jr., and Millstein, S. G., Correlates and predictors of risk-taking behavior during adolescence, in *Self-Regulatory Behavior and Risk Taking: Causes and Consequences* (L. P. Lipsitt and L. L. Mitnick, Eds.), Ablex, Norwood, New Jersey, 1991, pp. 2–21.
11. Caces, M. F., Stinson, F., and Harford, T., Alcohol use and physically risky behavior among adolescents, *Alcohol Health Res.* World 15:228–233 (1991).
12. Cobb, B., Cairns, B., Miles, M., et al., A longitudinal study of the role of sociodemographic factors and childhood aggression on adolescent injury and "close calls," *J. Adolesc. Health* 17:381–388 (1995).

13. Jelalian, E., Spirito, A., Rasile, D., et al., Risk-taking, self-reported injury, and perception of future injury in adolescents, *J. Pediatr. Psychol.* 22:513–532 (1997).

14. Starfield, B., Riley, A., Green, B., et al., The Adolescent Child Health and Illness Profile: a population-based measure of health, *Med. Care* 33:553–566 (1995).

15. Jessor, R., Donovan, J. E., and Costa, F. M., Problem drinking and risky driving among youth: a psychosocial approach to a lifestyle pattern, Proc. Int. Workshop: High Alcohol Consumers and Traffic (ACTes INRETS) 18:137–152 (1989).

16. Smith, R., Ptacek, J., and Smoll, F., Sensation seeking, stress, and adolescent injuries: a test of stress-buffering, risk-taking, and coping skills hypotheses, *J. Pets. Soc. Psychol.* 62:1016–1024 (1992).

17. Harrel, Y., Overpeck, M., Jones, D., et al., The effects of recall on estimating annual non-fatal injury rates for children and adolescents, *Am. J. Public Health* 84:599–601 (1994).

18. Katz, E., and Fromme, K., Alcohol and self-generated outcome expectancies for risk-taking, poster presented at the annual meeting of the Association for the Advancement of Behavior Therapy, New York, November 18, 1996.

16

Adolescence: Social and Emotional Development

Suicidal Behavior and Violence in Male Adolescents: A School-Based Study

Robert Vermeiren, Mary Schwab-Stone, Vladislav V. Ruchkin, Robert A. King, Cornelis Van Heeringen, and Dirk Deboutte

Objective: To investigate characteristics of suicidal and violent behavior in a community school sample of adolescents.

Method: Self-report questionnaires were administered to 794 male students (aged 12–18 years) from Antwerp, Belgium. Subjects were classified into four groups: a suicidal-only (n = 40; suicidal ideation and/or self-harming behavior), a violent-only (n = 142), a suicidal-violent (n = 21), and a control group (n = 591).

Results: Compared with controls, higher levels of internalizing problems, risk-taking behavior (substance use, diminished perception of risk, sensation seeking), and aggression were found in the comparison groups, The suicidal-violent group had the highest levels of depression, somatization, overt and covert aggression, and risk-taking behavior. Compared with the suicidal-only group, the violent-only group had less depression, anxiety, and covert aggression, but higher levels of overt aggression, sensation seeking, diminished perception of risk, and marijuana use.

Journal of the American Academy of Child and Adolescent Psychiatry, Jan 2003, v42, i1, p41(8).

© 2003 Lippincott/Williams & Wilkins.

Conclusions: Although adolescent suicidal and violent behavior are both related to internalizing problems, aggression, and risk-taking behavior, marked differences in severity and nature exist in these relationships. Differentiation of suicidal youths based on the presence or absence of violent behavior may add to our understanding of suicidal phenomena and may thus have important clinical consequences. J. Am. Acad. Child Adolesc. Psychiatry, *2003, 42(1):41–48.*

A strong body of literature has demonstrated an association between violent and/or antisocial and suicidal behavior (Plutchik and van Praag, 1997). Evidence for the association between both conditions in adolescents derives from different sources. First, psychological autopsy studies have found that the proportion of young suicides in which a disruptive behavior disorder could be diagnosed ranged from 20% to 50% (Brent et al., 1993; Marttunen et al., 1991; Shaffer et al., 1996). Second, epidemiological studies have shown that disruptive disorders are more prevalent in youthful suicide ideators and/or attempters than controls and that child and adolescent suicidal ideation and/or attempts are associated with violent and risk-taking behavior (e.g., substance use) (King et al., 2001; Orpinas et al., 1995; Sosin et al., 1995; Woods et al., 1997). Similarly, clinical studies have shown that youthful suicidal patients fairly often reveal histories of violent behavior (Cohen-Sandier et al., 1982), while others found aggression to be associated with repetition of attempted suicide in adolescents (Stein et al., 1998). Also, studies of incarcerated delinquent male youths have shown high prevalence rates of current suicidal ideation (13%-19%) (Morris et al., 1995; Rohde et al., 1997).

Further evidence for an association between suicidality and aggression comes from family aggregation studies (Botsis et al., 1995; Pfeffer et al., 1994), in which an increased level of antisocial and aggressive behavior in first-degree relatives of suicidal adolescents has been demonstrated. In addition, higher rates of aggression in young suicide victims have been related to higher loadings of suicide attempts in the family (Brent et al., 1996). Biological psychiatric research has demonstrated a pathogenetic role of serotonergic dysregulation in the development of both violent and suicidal behavior (Traskman-Bendz and Mann, 2000). However, the mechanisms that may determine the direction of aggression, i.e., inward or outward or both, still remain unclear.

An important line of research focuses specifically on the association between aggression and suicidal behavior. Although, as Plutchik and van Praag (1990) point out, the psychoanalytic idea that suicide reflects violence turned inward has some validity, it does not help us to understand why some aggressive people are suicidal while others are not. Consequently, Plutchik and van Praag (1997) developed a model that focuses specifically on the interconnection between violent and suicidal behavior. The model is based on evidence that aggression, described as an adaptive inner state, is influenced by a number of amplifiers and attenuators that may produce overt violence toward others or oneself. Plutchik and van Praag (1997) described almost 40 psychiatric, biological, personality-related, social, and familial variables as risk factors for violent behavior, of which more than half were also associated with an increased risk of suicidal behavior.

Apter et al. (1995) hypothesized that at least two types of suicidal behaviors can be discerned during adolescence. The first behavior reflects a wish to die and characterizes suicidal behavior in depressive disorders, while the second is characterized by impulse control problems and is commonly associated with externalizing disorders, such as conduct disorder. In a clinical sample of adolescents, Pfeffer et al. (1989) differentiated four groups based on the presence or absence of suicidal or assaultive behavior and found that, compared with controls, the group showing suicidal behavior was characterized by depression, drug use, and environmental stress, whereas the assaultive-only behavior group showed aggression and violence. The combined assaultive-suicidal behavior group showed both accidents and violence. Horesh et al. (1999) investigated the role of impulsivity and demonstrated a relationship between suicidal behavior and impulsivity, even after controlling for aggression.

Although of great importance for understanding the underlying mechanisms of suicide and violent behavior, the limitation of these studies was the almost exclusive reliance on clinical samples. Therefore, the current study aimed at examining suicidal and violent behavior in a community sample of adolescent students. This study was designed to examine and compare characteristics of youths with suicidal ideation/behavior only (suicidal-only), those with violent behavior only (violent-only), and those with histories of both suicidal ideation/behavior and violent behavior (suicidal-violent) with respect to internalizing problems, aggression, and risk-taking behavior. Suicidal adolescents were predicted to show primarily internalizing problems, risk-raking behavior, and some increase in aggression, while violent and combined violent-suicidal subjects were predicted to show increased aggression and risk-taking behavior.

METHOD

Sample

Subjects were adolescents participating in an ongoing cross-cultural project assessing risk and protective factors for adolescent adjustment. For this study, self-report surveys administered to a school sample of adolescents (aged 12–18 years) in Antwerp, Belgium, were used. Fifteen percent of the students were bsent on the day of administration. Of the surveyed group (N = 1,634), 125 subjects provided incomplete or inconsistent surveys and some classes

(77 students) did not complete the questionnaires used for this study, so that the total study group consisted of 1,432 students (male 794, female 638). Because of the very low prevalence of severe violent behavior in girls, analysis was confined to males.

The mean age of the participants was 14.9 (SD = 1.9). Ethnic distribution was as follows: 73.7%, native Belgian; 11.6%, Moroccan; 5.4%, Turkish; and 9.3%, others (mainly Southeast European and Central African). The study sample was representative of the general adolescent population of the Flemish part of Belgium with respect to unemployment (5.5% versus 5.0%) and parental education. Forty-four percent of the ethnic Flemish population had a high school diploma or higher (versus 45.1% for the population age category 35-64) (VRIND, 1999). Because most parents from other ethnic groups arrived in Belgium during adulthood, no comparison is available for this group.

Procedure

Data were collected in eight schools (middle and high school levels) in the city of Antwerp, Belgium, during the spring of 2000. Schools were chosen to represent different administrative school systems and different levels of education (Belgium has three main levels of education: professional, technical, and general). Intraclass correlation coefficients of the variables of interest were fair to good (bivariate correlation between schools: 0.54-0.87). Therefore, it was decided not to use school in the analyses. The survey was approved by the relevant boards of the school system, as well as those of the individual schools. Students and their parents were informed of the planned date of the survey administration. All students who were present on the day of administration were surveyed, unless they declined to participate or their parents had objections (eight individuals). Before starting the assessment, students signed assent forms, which included a statement of confidentiality. Concerning confidentiality, it w as noted that nobody (teachers, police, parents, or others) would ever know about the individual results of the respondent. The surveys were administered in the classrooms on a regular school day by trained personnel (psychologists, doctors, or medical students), who read all the questions aloud while students followed along, circling answers on their questionnaires. Questionnaires were in Dutch for all participants. Ten students reported language difficulties and were included in the noncompliant group.

Instruments

Socioeconomic Status. Parental education and current employment, as reported by the students, were used to assess socioeconomic status (SES). The parental education variable was transformed into three categories: did not complete high school, completed high school, and higher education. The current employment variable consisted of the categories no employment (0), industrial worker (1), employee (2), self-employed (3), and manager or professional (e.g., doctor, lawyer) (4). The final scores were added for adolescents reporting on both parents and doubled for those adolescents who reported that information regarding one of the parents was unavailable (e.g., because of death, being unknown). Doubling was done because the SES of one-parent families would otherwise be underestimated. Based on the final scores, five socioeconomic categories were created.

Delinquency Questionnaire. Violence items were derived from the self-report delinquency questionnaire of Junger-Tas (1994). Two interpersonal violence items were used to assess violent behavior during the past year: having threatened someone or having beaten someone up (Cronbach α = .82). Severity was assessed by asking the respondents about the frequency of each of these violent acts, using a 5-point scale (once, 2-4 times, more than 5 times, more than 10 times, or more than 20 times).

Suicidal Behavior. Questions derived from an unpublished questionnaire on child and adolescent self-harm (Child & Adolescent Self-harm in Europe, 2000) assessed the presence of suicidal ideation and deliberate self-harm during the past year. Suicidal ideation was assessed by asking whether a respondent had seriously thought about taking an overdose or harming himself, but did not do so. Deliberate self-harm was assessed by asking whether a respondent deliberately took an overdose of medication or tried to harm himself in some other way (e.g., cut himself). In addition, it was asked whether the participant had ever had the wish to die when deliberately harming himself (suicide attempt).

Behavior Assessment System for Children. Four scales from the Behavior Assessment System for Children were used to assess depressive symptoms, anxiety, somatization, and sensation seeking, using a true/false format (Reynolds and Kamphaus, 1992). The validity and reliability of this instrument have been widely documented, providing age-appropriate norms for each scale, and the instrument is being increasingly used internationally for assessment of psychopathology in children and adolescents. Four items on delinquent behavior (e.g., having a fight, stealing from a store) were excluded from the sensation seeking scale to ensure differentiation of sensation seeking from antisocial behavior constructs. Cronbach a values for the subscales in this population ranged from .60 for sensation seeking to .73 for depression.

Expectations About the Future. Five of the 10 items of Jessor's Expectations of Goal Attainment Scale (Jessor et al., 1989) were used to assess students' beliefs about their chances of achieving commonly accepted goals (i.e., chances that you will graduate from high school, will go to college, will have a job that pays well, will have a happy family life, will stay in good health most of the time). Cronbach α for this scale was .60.

Buss-Durkee Hostility Inventory—Dutch Version. The Buss-Durkee Hostility Inventory is a self-report questionnaire that has been translated and validated in the Dutch version by Lange et al. (1995). This instrument comprises three subscales assessing overt aggression, covert aggression, and social desirability. Whereas overt aggression consists of verbal and physical aggression toward others (i.e., "I never get so angry that I throw things"; "When I am angry, I slam doors"; "When I have to use violence to defend my rights, I will"), covert aggression can be characterized as a combination of hostility and suppressed anger (i.e., "I like to gossip"; "I am more often irritated than people know"; "I do not allow that little things bother me"). Cronbach a values for the scales were .74, .74, and .43, respectively.

Alcohol and Marijuana Use. Alcohol use was assessed by seven items derived from the Monitoring the Future Scale (Johnston et al., 1990). The instrument uses a 4-point frequency scale and includes six items that assess the use of three different alcoholic beverages (beer, wine, hard liquor; ever and during the past 30 days) and one item that assesses the frequency of binge drinking. All seven items were summed to obtain a total alcohol consumption score. Cronbach α for this scale was .91. Marijuana use was assessed by two questions, using a 4-point scale about the use of marijuana ever and during the past 30 days. Cronbach α for this scale was .89.

Diminished Perception of Risk. Ten items were used to assess the respondents' perception of risk of harming themselves if they were to engage in such activities as substance use, gun carrying, fighting, dropping our of school, and sexual intercourse without a condom. Four items were derived from the Monitoring the Future Scale (Johnston et al., 1990) and were further complemented by six additional items, drawn from the Social and Health Assessment, a school-based epidemiological instrument (Schwab-Stone et al., 1999). Choices on a 4-point scale ranged from no risk to great risk. Higher scores reflected diminished perception of the risk. The Cronbach α for this scale was .76.

Statistical Analysis

For statistical analysis, SPSS 10.0 was used. For all calculations, a was set at .05. First, groups were compared on demographic variables and the variables of interest by means of χ^2 and analysis of variance (ANOVA) tests. For ANOVA, post hoc pairwise comparisons were adjusted for multiple calculations with the Bonferroni procedure. Second, interaction between suicidal behavior and violence was tested with a series of univariate ANOVA (UNIANOVA) tests. Finally, logistic regression analyses were performed to analyze which variables predict group membership (suicidal-only versus violent-only, suicidal-only versus combined, violent-only versus combined). In the first step, SES, age, and race were entered simultaneously as adjusting variables. In the second step, all psychobehavioral variables were entered, and the best fit model was derived by using forward conditional selection.

RESULTS

Description of Comparison Groups

Based on the information on suicidal behavior and violence, four groups were distinguished. One hundred forty-two participants who committed more than one violent act during the past year but did not report suicidal ideation and/or deliberate self-harm formed the violent-only group (17.9%). The criterion of committing more than one violent act was used to include only the most severely and persistently violent adolescents. Forty participants reported suicidal ideation and/or deliberate self-harm during the past year but no severe violent behavior and formed the suicidal-only group (5.0%). Twenty-one participants reported suicidal ideation and/or deliberate self-harm and more than one violent act during the past year and were considered as the combined or the suicidal-violent group (2.6%). Finally, students who did not report suicidal ideation and/or deliberate self-harm and who did nor commit more than one violent act during the past year were considered as the control group (n = 591; 74.4%).

Sociodemographic Characteristics and Suicide Attempts

Sociodemographic variables for all four groups are presented in Table 1. Age did not differ significantly across groups. Both the violent-only and the suicidal-violent group came from significantly lower socioeconomic classes. Also, subjects from these two groups tended to live more frequently in single-parent households, while significantly more violent-only subjects had changed schools since they started high school. Minority youths were overrepresented in the violent-only group.

Suicide attempts ever (the wish to die when harming himself) was more than twice as prevalent in the combined group when compared with the suicidal-only group, a finding that was significant.

Internalizing Problems

Compared with controls, all other groups revealed significantly higher rates of depression and somatization, while the suicidal-only group showed the highest ratings of anxiety and the lowest scores with regard to expectations for the future. Compared with the violent-only subjects, suicidal-only subjects showed more depression, anxiety, and a trend toward lower expectations about the future. The combined group was similar to the suicidal-only group, although a trend toward lower anxiety was present, and the combined group differed from the violent-only group on depression and somatization.

Aggression

All groups had higher levels of overt and covert aggression than controls, although the difference between the suicidal-only group and controls did not

TABLE 1. Sociodemographic Characteristics and Suicide Attempts by Group

	CONTROL (n = 591)	SUICIDAL-ONLY (n = 40)
Mean (SD) age	15.09 (1.96)	15.35 (2.12)
Mean (SD) SES (b,c)	2.93 (1.27)	3.29 (1.106)
No. (%) minority (b)	132 (22.4)	4 (10.0)
No. (%) single-parent family	97 (16.4)	6 (15.0)
No. (%) of students who changed School (b)	228 (38.6)	12 (30.0)
No. (%) suicide attempts (ever) (a,c)	0 (0.0)	12 (30.0)
	VIOLENT-ONLY (n = 142)	SUICIDAL-VIOLENT (n = 21)
Mean (SD) age	15.27 (1.70)	15.48 (2.11)
Mean (SD) SES (b,c)	2.36 (1.26)	2.05 (1.15)
No. (%) minoriry (b)	61 (43.0)	4 (19.0)
No. (%) single-parent family	31 (21.8)	6 (28.6)
No. (%) of students who changed School (b)	83 (58.5)	9 (42.9)
No. (%) suicide attempts (ever) (a,c)	0 (0.0)	14 (66.7)
	F; p	
Mean (SD) age	NS	
Mean (SD) SES (b,c)	F = 11.8 ***	
No. (%) minoriry (b)	χ^2 = 31.5***	
No. (%) single-parent family	NS	
No. (%) of students who changed School (b)	χ^2 = 21.0***	
No. (%) suicide attempts (ever) (a,c)	χ^2 = 381.5***	

Note: NS = not significant; SES = socioeconomic status.
(a) Significant difference between control and suicidal-only.
(b) Significant difference between control and violent-only.
(c) Significant difference between control and suicidal-violent.
***p < .001.

reach significance for overt aggression. Compared with the violent-only group, the suicidal-only group was significantly higher in covert aggression and lower in overt aggression. The combined group was high on both overt and covert aggression and differed from the suicidal-only group in overt aggression and from the violent-only group in covert aggression.

Risk-Taking Behavior and Sensation Seeking

When compared with controls, the suicidal-only and the combined groups more commonly reported alcohol use, whereas the violent-only and the combined groups reported higher levels of sensation seeking, diminished perception of risk, and marijuana use. The violent-only and the combined groups differed from the suicidal-only group in having a diminished perception of risk and more sensation seeking and marijuana use.

Interaction Between Suicidal Behavior and Violent Behavior

By means of a series of UNIANOVAs, the interaction between suicidal behavior and violent behavior in predicting the outcome variables was analyzed. Inadequate power (< 0.8) was obtained for all calculations but one (diminished perception of risk). For diminished perception of risk, a significant interaction effect was found ($F_{1,779} = 9.2$; $p < .01$). Table 2 shows that a diminished perception of risk was at a similar level in both the control and the suicidal-only group, slightly higher in the violent-only group, but considerably higher in the combined group. A significant interaction effect was also present for anxiety ($F_{1,788} = 6.2$; $p < .05$). Anxiety was significantly higher in the suicidal-only group when compared with both the control group and the violent-only group (with similar anxiety levels in those groups), while no such increase was present for the combined group (Table 2).

Logistic Regression

When compared with violent-only group status, suicidal-only group status was best predicted by higher levels of covert aggression and lower levels of overt aggression, marijuana use, and diminished perception of risk (Table 3). Combined group status, when compared with suicidal-only group status, was best predicted by higher levels of sensation seeking and diminished perception of risk. When compared with violent-only, combined group status was best predicted by higher levels of somatization, sensation seeking, and diminished perception of risk.

DISCUSSION

This community study of adolescents supports previous findings (Plutchik and van Praag, 1997) that suicidal and violent subjects share characteristics related to aggressive tendencies and risk-taking behavior. However, the nature of these characteristics differs across groups; the suicidal-only subjects show more covert aggression and alcohol use, while the violent-only subjects show more overt aggression, sensation seeking, and marijuana use. Contrary to the expected results, when compared with controls, all three comparison groups showed more depression and somatization, although these problems were most apparent in the suicidal-only group. Finally, the combined group differed substantially from the suicidal-only group on overt aggression, sensation seeking, perception of risk, and substance use, supporting the idea that distinct subgroups of suicidal youths can be distinguished on the basis of the level of violence.

Table 2. Means (SD) of Internalizing Problems, Aggression, and Risk-Taking Behavior by Group

	Control (n = 591)	Suicidal-Only (n = 40)	Violent Only (n = 142)	Suicidal Violent (n = 21)	Post Hoc Comparisons	F (df); p
Depression	1.72 (2.0)	4.30 (3.5)	2.66 (2.5)	4.76 (3.1)	a,b,c,d,f	31.4 (3,788)***
Anixiety	5.08 (3.0)	8.03 (3.5)	5.18 (2.9)	6.01 (2.8)	a,d	12.5 (3,788)***
Somatization	1.53 (1.5)	2.81 (2.2)	2.24 (1.7)	3.68 (2.4)	a,b,c,f	23.6 (3,788)***
Expectations about the future	15.82 (2.2)	14.60 (2.9)	15.64 (2.7)	15.19 (3.5)	a	3.6 (3,778)*
Overt aggression	8.93 (3.1)	10.10 (2.9)	11.61 (2.3)	12.57 (2.3)	b,c,d,e	40.5 (3,790)***
Covert aggression	8.10 (3.7)	12.13 (3.1)	10.20 (3.4)	12.67 (3.0)	a,b,c,d,f	33.5 (3,790)***
Diminished perception of risk	17.03 (4.2)	17.93 (5.5)	21.12 (5.8)	26.05 (5.8)	b,c,d,e,f	49.9 (3,779)***
Sensation seeking	5.71 (2.4)	6.41 (2.6)	7.58 (1.8)	8.85 (1.4)	b,c,d,e	36.3 (3,788)***
Alcohol use	14.28 (6.2)	17.26 (5.8)	15.74 (7.4)	21.80 (5.9)	a,c,f	12.1 (3,773)***
Marijuana use	3.11 (2,0)	3.43 (2.2)	4.46 (2.6)	5.14 (2.4)	b,c,d,e	20.4 (3,788)***

Note: Post hoc comparisons between subgroups corrected with Bonferroni adjustment for multiple calculations.
(a) Significant difference between control and suicidal-only.
(b) Significant difference between control and violent-only.
(c) Significant difference between control and suicidal-violent.
(d) Siginificant difference between suicidal-only and violent-only.
(e) Significant difference between suicidal-only and suicidal-violent.
(f) Significant difference between violent-only and suicidal-violent.
*$p < .05$
***$p < .001$.

Table 3. Logistic Regression, Variables Predicting Group Member Status (Adjusted for Age, Socioeconomic Status, and Race)

	B	OR (95% CI)	p
Dependent: suicidal-only/violent-only			
Covert aggression	−0.37	0.69 (0.58–0.82)	.00
Overt aggression	0.24	1.26 (1.04–1.54)	.02
Marijuana use	0.25	1.28 (1.00–1.64)	.05
Diminished perception of risk	0.12	1.13 (1.02–1.25)	.02
Overall model: χ^2 =73.4, Cox & Snell R^2 = 0.34			
Dependent: suicidal-only/combined			
Sensation seeking	0.95	2.58 (1.19–5.56)	.02
Diminished perception of risk	0.25	1.29 (1.09–1.52)	.00
Overall model: χ^2 = 42.2, Cox & Snell R^2 = 0.52			
Dependent: violent-only/combined			
Somatization	0.30	1.36 (1.03–1.78)	.03
Sensation seeking	0.52	1.68 (1.11–2.55)	.01
Diminished perception of risk	0.13	1.14 (1.03–1.27)	.02
Overall model: $\chi^2 6$ = 34.8, Cox & Snell R^2 = 0.20			

Note: OR = odds ratio
CI = confidence interval.

Summarizing the specific characteristics of each group, one may describe the suicidal-only group as mainly anxious/depressed, and high in covert aggression and in alcohol use; the violent-only group as high in somatization, overt aggression, and severe substance use; and the combined group as high in depression/somatization, both covert and overt aggression, and all forms of risk-taking behavior. With regard to aggression, future research should investigate whether differences in overt versus covert aggression arise from differential influences of attenuators and amplifiers, as described earlier by Plutchik and van Praag (1997).

The current study found few differences between the suicidal-only and the control group on risk-raking behavior. Taken alone, the suicidal-only group does not appear to manifest what Holinger (1979) suggested as a continuum of self destructiveness," ranging from the covert (e.g., substance use, unprotected and precocious sexual activity) to the overt (e.g., self-mutilation and suicide attempts). This finding, however, may be due to the differentiation of the suicidal-only group from the suicidal-violent group, in which risk-taking behavior was much higher. Considering suicidal individuals as just one group (including violent subjects) would substantially increase the apparent association between risk-raking behavior and suicidality. The profound differences between the suicidal-only and the combined group in the current study underline the importance of keeping in mind these differences in future research and in clinical and preventive interventions. Differences in sensation seeking may as well explain the higher number of past suicide attempts in the combined group when compared with the suicidal-only group. Sensation seeking is related to impulsivity; a known risk factor for actual suicidal behavior (Horesh et al., 1999).

The high level of risk-taking behavior in both the combined and the violent-only groups is not surprising, as violent youths often are involved in a delinquent subculture as part of their behavior. Conversely, suicidal adolescents show higher levels of anxiety, which might decrease their tendency toward hazardous or delinquent behavior, while perhaps predisposing toward alcohol use.

The findings with regard to depression and somatization, which gradually increase in severity from the control group through the violent-only group, the suicidal-only group, and finally the combined group, correspond to increases in covert aggression. This is expected, as an association between covert aggression and internalizing problems has been demonstrated (Lange et al., 1995). As the underlying mechanism for this association remains unresolved, it will be important to investigate whether internalizing problems have any influence on the qualitative development of aggression or the reverse, as this may be critically important for an individual's behavioral outcome and may potentially represent a critical intervention focus.

The present findings suggesting impoverished minority background and frequent change of school as risk factors for violence are in keeping with previous studies on the factors predisposing to violence (Patterson et al., 1998). Minority youths were disproportionately represented in the violent groups. This striking finding may well result from the association between minority status, SES, and violence, with four fifths of minorities belonging to the lowest socioeconomic group. In the Belgian context, where the parents of minority youths commonly are recent immigrants, minority status serves as a marker for differences in socioeconomic, language, acculturation, immigration, and exposure to violence.

Clinical Implications

Differentiation of suicidal youths based on the presence or absence of violent behavior may add to our understanding of the suicidal phenomena in adolescents and may have important clinical consequences. Apart from screening for depression as an efficient strategy in the prevention of suicide in children and adolescents at risk (Shaffer and Craft, 1999), an adequate assessment of violent behavior and risk-raking behavior may also be helpful.

Taking together the characteristics of the suicidal-only, the violent-only, and the combined groups, it is evident that all groups are in need of multifaceted intervention. The combined group in particular requires intense clinical attention, especially because a higher number of actual suicide attempts may occur in this group. Also, because the suicidal-only and the combined suicidal-violent groups appeared substantially different, it is likely that specific therapeutic interventions will be needed for each of these suicidal subgroups.

Limitations

Some limitations of the study need to be noted. First, the cross-sectional nature of the study does not allow conclusions about etiological pathways. Second, all information was derived from self-report surveys, and even though it has been demonstrated that self-reports can be used reliably for the assessment of behavioral problems (JungerTas, 1994; Rutter et al., 1998), the impact of factors such as inconsistency of answering and social desirability cannot be fully excluded. As most severe violent behavior is uncommon in community samples (Plutchik and van Praag, 1990), epidemiological research by means of self-report instruments is needed. Third, no information was available on the nonparticipants, making it impossible to compare them with participants. Also, because this was a school-based survey, assessments could only be done with adolescents attending school. Future research should attempt to include out-of-school students and to investigate in what way they differ from participants, as these absent youths may present with more problems (and experience greater levels of violence) than participating youths. Fourth, the combined suicidal-violent group in particular was low in number, which may have reduced the power to detect interaction effects. Fifth, the suicidal-only and the combined groups include both suicidal ideation and/or self-harming behavior during the past year. Due to the relatively low frequency of suicidal behavior, further differentiation of suicidal groups was not feasible and should be a focus of future research. Because the assessment of suicide attempts (self-harming behavior and the wish to die) was not specified in time, the number of participants who attempted suicide during the past year cannot be determined. Suicide attempts occurred more often in the combined group when compared with the suicidal-only group, which may have influenced the results. Finally, the study was conducted in just one Western city, and one should be cautious when generalizing the findings to other cultures.

This article was written when the first author was Belgian American Educational Foundation Research Fellow in the Yale Child Study Center. The authors appreciate the support of the Hewlett Foundation for the Yale Child Study Program on International Child Mental Health. The authors gratefully acknowledge the support and helpful guidance of Donald J. Cohen, M.D., the late Director, Yale Child Study Center.

CRITICAL THINKING QUESTIONS

1. Compare and contrast the control group and "experimental" groups in terms of race, risk-taking, and psychiatric issues. What conclusions can be drawn from this information?

2. What are the "real-life" implications of this research? How do you think parents, teachers, and health care providers could use this information to provide interventions for suicidal adolescents?
3. What new information did you learn by reading this article? Was there any information that surprised you?

REFERENCES

Apter A, Gothelf D, Orbach I et al. (1995), Correlation of suicidal and violent behavior in different diagnostic categories in hospitalized adolescent patients. *J Am Acad Child Adolesc* Psychiatry 34:912–918

Botsis AJ, Plutchik R, Koder M, van Praag HM (1995), Parental loss and family violence as correlates of suicide and violence risk. *Suicide Life Threat Behav* 25:253–260

Brent DA, Bridge J, Johnson BA, Connolly J (1996), Suicidal behavior runs in families: a controlled family study of adolescent suicide victims. *Arch Gen Psychiatry* 53:1145–1152

This article was written when the first author was Belgian American Educational Foundation Research Fellow in the Yale Child Study Center. The authors appreciate the support of the Hewlett Foundation for the Yale Child Study Program on International Child Mental Health. The authors gratefully acknowledge the support and helpful guidance of Donald J. Cohen, M.D., the late Director, Yale Child Study Center.

Brent DA, Perper JA, Moritz C et al. (1993), Psychiatric risk factors for adolescent suicide: a case-control study. *J Am Acad Child Adolesc Psychiatry* 32:521–529

Child & Adolescent Selfharm in Europe (2000), Lifestyle and Coping Questionnaire (unpublished study questionnaire). London: National Children's Bureau (www.selfharm.org.uk)

Cohen-Sandler R, Berman AL. King RA (1982), Life stress and symptomatology: determinants of suicidal behavior in children. *J Am Acad Child Psychiatry* 21:178–186

Holinger PC (1979), Violent deaths among the young: recent trends in suicide, homicide, and accidents. *Am J Psychiatry* 136:1144–1147

Horesh N, Cothelf D, Ofek H, Weizman T, Apter A (1999), Impulsivity as a correlate of suicidal behavior in adolescent psychiatric inpatients. *Crisis* 20:8–14

Jessor R, Donovan JE, Costa FM (1989), *School Health Study.* Boulder: Institute of Behavioral Science, University of Colorado

Johnston LD, Bachman J, O'Malley PM (1990), *Monitoring the Future.* Ann Arbor: Institute for Social Research, University of Michigan (www.monitoringthefuture.org)

Junger-Tas (1994), *Delinquent Behaviour Among Young People in the Western World*. Amsterdam/New York: Kugler Publications

King RA, Schwab-Stone M, Flisher AJ et al, (2001), Psychosocial and risk behavior correlates of youth suicide attempts and suicidal ideation. *J Am Acad Child Adolesc Psychiatry* 40:837–846

Lange A, Dehghani B, de Beurs E (1995), Validation of the Dutch adaptation of the Buas-Durkee Hostility Inventory. *Behav Res Ther* 33:229–233

Marttunen MJ, Aro HM, Henriksson MM, Lonnqvist JK (1991), Mental disorders in adolescent suicide: DSM-III-R Axes I and II diagnoses in suicides among 13-to 19-year-olds in Finland. *Arch Gen Psychiatry* 48:834–839

Morris RE, Harrison EA, Knox GW, Tromanhauser E, Marquis DK, Watts LL (1995), Health risk behavioral survey from 39 juvenile correctional facilities in the United States. *J Adolest Health* 17:334–344

Orpinas PK, Basen-Engquist K, Grunbaum JA, Parcel CS (1995), The co-morbidity of violence-related behaviors with health-risk behaviors in a population of high school students. *J Adolesc Health* 16:216–225

Patterson CR, Forgatch MS, Yoerger KL, Stoolmiller M (1998), Variables that initiate and maintain an early-onset trajectory for juvenile offending. *Dev Psychopathol* 10:531–547

Pfeffer CR, Newcorn J, Kaplan C, Mizruchi MS. Plutchik R (1989), Subtypes of suicidal and assaultive behaviors in adolescent psychiatric inpatients: a research note. *J Child Psychol Psychiatry* 30:151–163

Pfeffer CR, Normandin L, Kakuma T (1994), Suicidal children grow up: suicidal behavior and psychiatric disorders among relatives. *J Am Acad Child Adolest Psychiatry* 33:1087–1097

Plutchik R, van Praag HM (1990), Psychosocial correlates of suicide and violence risk In: *Violence and Suicidality: Perspectives in Clinical and Psychobiological Research* (Clinical and Experimental Psychiatry Monograph, 3), van Praag HM, Plutchik R, Apter A, eds. New York: Brunner/Mazel, pp 37–65

Plutchik R, van Praag HM (1997), Suicide, impulsivity, and antisocial behavior. In: *Handbook of Antisocial Behavior*, Stoff DM, Breiling J, Maser JD, eds. New York: Wiley, pp 101–108

Reynolds CR, Kamphaus RW (1992), *BASC Behavior Assessment System for Children Manual*. Circle Pines, MN: American Guidance Service

Rohde P, Seeley JR, Mace DE (1997), Correlates of suicidal behavior in a juvenile detention population. *Suicide Life Threat Behav* 27:164–175

Rutter M, Giller H, Hagell A (1998), *Antisocial Behavior by Young People*. New York: Cambridge University Press

Schwab-Stone M, Chen C, Greenberger E, Silver D, Lichtman J, Voyce C (1999), No safe haven, II: the effects of violence exposure on urban youth. *J Am Acad Child Adolesc Psychiatry* 38:359–367

Shaffer D, Craft L (1999), Methods of adolescent suicide prevention. *J Clin Psychiatry* 60(suppl 2):70–74

Shaffer D, Gould MS, Fisher Pet al. (1996), Psychiatric diagnosis in child and adolescent suicide. *Arch Gen Psychiatry* 53:339–348

Sosin DM, Koepsell TD, Rivara FP, Mercy JA (1995), Fighting as a marker for multiple problem behaviors in adolescents. *J Adolesc Health* 16:209–215

Stein D, Apter A, Ratzoni G, Har-Even D, Avidan G (1998), Association between multiple suicide attempts and negative affects in adolescents. *J Am Acad Child Adolesc* Psychiatry 37:488–494

Traskman-Bendz L, Mann JJ (2000), Biological aspects of suicidal behaviour. In: *International Handbook of Suicide and Attempted Suicide*, Hawton K, Van Heeringen K, eds. Chichester: Wiley

VRIND (1999), *Vlaamse Regionale Indicatoren* (Flemish Regional Indicators). Brussels: Vlaamse Gemeenschap (Flemish Community)

Woods ER, Lin YG, Middleman A, Beckford P, Chase L, DuRant RH (1997), The associations of suicide attempts in adolescents. *Pediatrics* 99:791–796

From the University Department of Child and Adolescent Psychiatry, Middelheimhospital, University of Antwerp, Belgium (Drs. Vermeiren and Deboutte); Yale Child Study Center, New Haven, CT (Drs. Schwab-Stone, Ruchkin, and King); and Unit for Suicide Research, University of Ghent, Belgium (Dr. Van Heeringen).

InfoMarks: Make Your Mark

What Is an InfoMark?

It's a single-click return ticket to any page, any result, any search from InfoTrac College Edition.

An InfoMark is a stable URL, linked to InfoTrac College Edition articles that you have selected. InfoMarks can be used like any other URL, but they're better because they're stable—they don't change. Using an InfoMark is like performing the search again whenever you follow the link—whether the result is a single article or a list of articles.

How Do InfoMarks Work?

If you can "copy and paste," you can use InfoMarks.

When you see the InfoMark icon on a result page, its URL can be copied and pasted into your electronic document—Web page, word processing document, or email. Once InfoMarks are incorporated into a document, the results are persistent (the URLs will not change) and are dynamic.

Even though the saved search is used at different times by different users, an InfoMark always functions like a brand new search. Each time a saved search is executed, it accesses the latest updated information. That means subsequent InfoMark searches might yield additional or more up-to-date information than the original search with less time and effort.

Capabilities

InfoMarks are the perfect technology tool for creating:

- Virtual online readers
- Current awareness topic sites—links to periodical or newspaper sources
- Online/distance learning courses
- Bibliographies, reference lists
- Electronic journals and periodical directories
- Student assignments
- Hot topics

Advantages

- Select from over 15 million articles from more than 5,000 journals and periodicals
- Update article and search lists easily
- Articles are always full-text and include bibliographic information
- All articles can be viewed online, printed, or emailed
- Saves professors and students time
- Anyone with access to InfoTrac College Edition can use it
- No other online library database offers this functionality
- FREE!

How to Use InfoMarks

There are three ways to utilize InfoMarks—in HTML documents, Word documents, and email

HTML Document

1. Open a new document in your HTML editor (Netscape Composer or FrontPage Express).
2. Open a new browser window and conduct your search in InfoTrac College Edition.
3. Highlight the URL of the results page or article that you would like to InfoMark.
4. Right click the URL and click Copy. Now, switch back to your HTML document.
5. In your document, type in text that describes the InfoMarked item.
6. Highlight the text and click on Insert, then on Link in the upper bar menu.
7. Click in the link box, then press the "Ctrl" and "V" keys simultaneously and click OK. This will paste the URL in the box.
8. Save your document.

Word Document

1. Open a new Word document.
2. Open a new browser window and conduct your search in InfoTrac College Edition.
3. Check items you want to add to your Marked List.
4. Click on Mark List on the right menu bar.
5. Highlight the URL, right click on it, and click Copy. Now, switch back to your Word document.
6. In your document, type in text that describes the InfoMarked item.

7. Highlight the text. Go to the upper bar menu and click on Insert, then on Hyperlink.
8. Click in the hyperlink box, then press the "Ctrl" and "V" keys simultaneously and click OK. This will paste the URL in the box.
9. Save your document.

Email

1. Open a new email window.
2. Open a new browser window and conduct your search in InfoTrac College Edition.
3. Highlight the URL of the results page or article that you would like to InfoMark.
4. Right click the URL and click Copy. Now, switch back to your email window.
5. In the email window, press the "Ctrl" and "V" keys simultaneously. This will paste the URL into your email.
6. Send the email to the recipient. By clicking on the URL, he or she will be able to view the InfoMark.